WELCOME HOME, BROTHER

WELCOME HOME, BROTHER

Memoirs of Vietnam War Veterans

Michel Robertson

Foreword by Lt. Gen. John M. Brown III
US Army (Ret.)

Copyright © 2019 Michel Robertson

All rights reserved.

Front cover, left to right:
Peter Lillard, Clark Murray, Flynn Trimnal

Back cover, top to bottom:
Dave Grant, Howard Thiele, Mike Di Rocco
Clyde Jones, David Morrow, Ray Pavlik

ISBN   9781708229665

Printed in the United States of America by Kindle Direct Publishing

Cover Design: Advertising PLUS, Lawrenceville, Georgia
adplus@mac.com

This book is for sale on Amazon.com.

All proceeds from this book benefit
the Veterans History Museum of the Carolinas &
the Vietnam Veterans of America (VVA), Asheville Chapter #124.

Bonded by the unspeakable horrors of war
and by their country's lack of gratitude upon their return home,
Vietnam War veterans acknowledge their shared experiences
and greet each other with the words their countrymen forgot:
Welcome Home, Brother.

Dedication

This book is dedicated to all Vietnam era veterans who bore the trials of a nation mired in bitter debate; and especially to those men and women who served in-country.

Unlike WWII veterans, whose return from war was embraced with gratitude and parades, Vietnam War veterans suffered indifference, rejection, and contempt. Their stories illuminate their service and preserve the history of their sacrifice. It is never too late to honor them. There is still time to say, *Welcome Home, Brothers and Sisters.*

Michel Robertson
December 2019

Acknowledgments

This book took shape over two years and was made possible through the efforts of many people.

Thank you, John Lanier, editor of the *Transylvania Times,* for the biweekly publication of thirty-one Vietnam War veterans' memoirs. You took a risk on this venture and changed lives because of it.

To my friends. Johnny Martinez, your commitment to helping veterans inspired me to embark upon this project. Mike McCarthy, thank you for advocating this series and for challenging me to get it done when I flagged. Janis Allen, countless thanks for tutoring me through the frustrations and vagaries of self-publishing. David Morrow, your comments on the back cover of this book make my heart swell; and General John Brown, your eloquent and heartfelt *Foreword* captures the essence of this two-year project.

Thank you, Hale Irwin, for your postscript to the story of Ray Alcorn.

To my husband and Vietnam War veteran, Bill Robertson, thank you for tolerating Lean Cuisines, postponed vacations, and a grumpy wife as I labored over biweekly newspaper articles; and for reading and editing each account and correcting my military gaffes. You're my rock.

I have the highest regard for two organizations that honor the service and sacrifices of our veterans: the Veterans History Museum of the Carolinas (Emmett Casciato, Founder and Curator) and the Vietnam Veterans of America, Asheville Chapter #124. All profits from the sale of this book will be donated to these two deserving organizations.

Finally, to the Vietnam veterans featured in this collection, thank you for your courageous return to a place and time when you put everything on the line for a country that looked the other way. You have my respect and friendship forever.

CONTENTS

Dedication	vii
Acknowledgments	ix
Foreword	xiii
Introduction	xv
Michael Di Rocco: *Living with the Montagnards*	1
David Crandal: *USMC During the Early War Years*	7
Andrew W. Boyko: *Two Eras, Two Kinds of Warfare*	11
James Clark Murray: *Big Guns on the Ho Chi Minh Trail*	17
Clyde Jones: *The Big E – A Recipe for Success*	25
Howard Thiele: *Vietnam from the Driver's Seat*	33
Wendell "Ray" Alcorn: *Seven Years a Prisoner of War*	39
Ray Pavlik: *Choreography on the Deck of the Kittyhawk*	53
James G. McKinney: *Artilleryman Travelling with The Big Red One*	59
Purvis James Boatwright, Jr.: *Supporting Marines on the Ground*	65
Joe T. Smith: *Under Attack at Home and Abroad*	69
John K. Barker: *Flying F-4 Phantoms Over Hanoi*	73
Ervin P. Bridges: *Walking to War*	81
William E. Robertson: *Seabees 'Can Do' Motto Tested in Vietnam*	89

Joseph A. Sansosti: *The Fiercely Fought Battle of Dai Do*	93
Michael D. Kuhne: *A View from the Tonkin Gulf*	101
John "Larry" McCall: *Securing the Mekong Delta*	107
Curtiss L. Poteat: *Patrolling the Rivers of South Vietnam*	111
Louis P. Mayrand, Jr.: *Army Ranger's Last Mission in Vietnam*	117
C. G. "Jug" Gerard: *From Jet Jockey to Helicopters*	123
David P. Morrow: *Seabees Building Relationships*	131
Richard G. Woodhull: *Flying Spy Planes Over Vietnam*	139
Ronald Severs: *Marine Combat Engineer*	147
Johnny Martinez: *Lessons I Learned from the Vietnam War*	155
Phil Seymour: *The Night of the Spiders*	161
Grady L. Jackson: *Fighting the War from the Air*	169
Steve Salsburg: *On Board as a U.S. Naval Flight Surgeon*	179
David Smale: *Scramble the Seawolves*	187
Peter T. Lillard: *A New Concept in Amphibious Warfare*	195
Earl "Flynn" Trimnal: *War in the Tunnels of Vietnam*	203
David B. Grant: *F-4 Phantom Pilot and Prisoner of War*	213

CONTENTS (alphabetized)

Alcorn, Ray 39
Barker, John 73
Boatwright, James 65
Boyko, Andy 11
Bridges, Ervin 81
Crandal, David 7
Di Rocco, Mike 1
Gerard, Jug 123
Grant, Dave 213
Jackson, Grady 169
Jones, Clyde 25
Kuhne, Mike 101
Lillard, Peter 195
Martinez, Johnny 155
Mayrand, Phil 117
McCall, Larry 107
McKinney, Jimmy 59
Morrow, David 131
Murray, Clark 17
Pavlik, Ray 53
Poteat, Curtiss 111
Robertson, Bill 89
Salsburg, Steve 179
Sansosti, Joe 93
Severs, Ron 147
Seymour, Phil 161
Smale, David 187
Smith, Joe 69
Thiele, Sarge 33
Trimnal, Flynn 203
Woodhull, Duke 139

Foreword

They stepped forward. Like their fathers, mothers, grandparents, uncles, big brothers and neighbors, they stepped forward to serve and protect their country. They did not pick their war; that was done by the nation's leaders and circumstance. Some volunteered, some were drafted but they all served and did their duty. Their stories are real, coming from deep and often raw memories of their brothers and sisters in uniform, their fears and their pride. They remember friends, losses and triumphs. They remember family support, sacrifice and the terrible toll on Americans and Vietnamese. Their memories and stories are powerful and historic treasures.

They remember being surprised at the anger turned toward them by many Americans as the war became increasingly unpopular. Rather than political and military leaders, *they* became the focal point of antiwar sentiment across the nation. For the first time in our history, American citizens blamed our soldiers for the war. We the People failed our warriors. Some actively attacked our soldiers as they came home. Many stood by and let it happen. We lessened our national character at the expense of those who served. Their strength in the face of these unwarranted attacks taught the nation a lesson that is also part of their service to country. A lesson we must never forget and must pass to our children: in a democracy, it is OK to hate a war and still respect the soldiers sent into battle. We should share pride in the veterans described in this collection. Bless them.

Lieutenant General John M Brown III
U.S. Army (Retired)

Introduction

My personal connection with the war in Vietnam began as a high school student in 1968 when my friend Jean and I prepared a CARE package for Vietnam War veterans, stuffing it with beef jerky, hard candy, and James Bond paperbacks. At the last minute, Jean's older sister produced her contribution: a copy of *The Pilgrim's Progress*, a Christian allegory written in 1687 in Old English. Imagine a battle-weary soldier in his hooch, struggling through a 200-year-old account of a good man's pilgrimage through life!

This book's "pilgrimage" began in Brevard, North Carolina, when, after attending a WWII veteran's funeral service which included a military ceremony, I decided to write an article about the Transylvania County Honor Guard for our local newspaper. As I met and talked with Vietnam veterans, I revisited memories of the turbulent 1960's and 70's, when boys my age were drafted or enlisted, some coming home in body bags; all of them returning altered in some way. Anger over an increasingly unwinnable war divided our country and resentment of the government by some found its outlet in our men and women in uniform.

1968 to 1972: Vietnam on a College Campus

During the late 1960's, Americans experienced an unprecedented phenomenon — war footage introduced into their homes via television. Vietnam was nicknamed *the living room war*. Journalists weren't required to submit their stories to military censors for clearance as they had been during World War II and the Korean War. Nightly news reports included uncensored images of death, brutality and casualties on both sides -- disturbing scenes to American civilians who had never experienced military conflict.

A midwestern child of the Chicago suburbs, I arrived at Smith College in Massachusetts unprepared for the political unrest and activism of an eastern college. I respected the veterans in my family, especially my father, but I also came to believe that we should not have become involved in Vietnam. My father, a WWII Army Air Corps navigator in the Pacific, made his feelings clear when he told me, "I believe in freedom of speech and in your right to voice your opinions. But, if I see you carrying an anti-war placard on the nightly news, you're paying for your own education." I toed the line.

When I graduated, the war in Vietnam was winding down as President Nixon pursued a policy of withdrawal and de-escalation. As our combatants returned from war, I assumed they would re-integrate into American life. Meanwhile, with diploma in hand, I moved to Washington, D.C., and faced the predictable challenges of landing a job with a degree in Early Modern European History.

Of course, hindsight has taught us that Vietnam veterans did *not* easily re-assimilate. But in 1973, after the longest war in this country's history to-date, our war-weary and divided nation longed for closure; and, in the process, we abandoned our warriors.

Learning New Lessons

Forty-five years later, as I interviewed Vietnam War veterans for an Honor Guard article, I realized that many continue to suffer from flashbacks, nightmares, and guilt. I understood my culpability in the treatment of the returning veterans of my generation: inattention. I needed to face the inadequacies of my past; but what could I do for veterans whom we abandoned so long ago? All I could think of was to record their stories.

After presenting my idea to Emmett Casciato, Curator and Founder of the Veterans History Museum of the Carolinas, we approached John Lanier, editor of the *Transylvania Times* newspaper, who suggested that over the course of a year I submit biweekly articles featuring Transylvania County Vietnam War veterans who served in-country. I was overwhelmed at the enormity of the task. Could I find twenty-six veterans willing to share their stories?

To the credit of every veteran interviewed, I was treated with respect, patience and generosity. There was no shortage of subjects, and twelve months became sixteen. In the process, we forged lasting friendships.

Unexpected Results

To my surprise, there were important and unanticipated consequences. As they relived and discussed their experiences, many veterans found a measure of relief and closure not experienced since their return from war. My husband, a Navy Seabee based near the demilitarized zone, described experiences for the first time in thirty years of marriage. Wives and children told me, "I've never heard any of this," and, "This helped our entire family." One veteran wrote, "My universe has shifted because of this endeavor." Another soldier explained, "My son was amazed when he read my story. Our relationship has changed because of it." The newspaper stories also encouraged *other* veterans to initiate conversations with their families on topics suppressed for decades.

There are no stories of female veterans in this collection for the simple reason that I could not locate any such veterans in our county. To you who were there I say, "Welcome home, sisters."

A pilgrimage, loosely defined, is a long journey taken to pay homage. In the process, I arrived at a better understanding and appreciation of our country's servicemen and women and the unimaginable sacrifices they make on our behalf.

Michel Johns and her father, Larry Johns, 1973

Michel Johns Roberton, 2019

AREA OF OPERATIONS

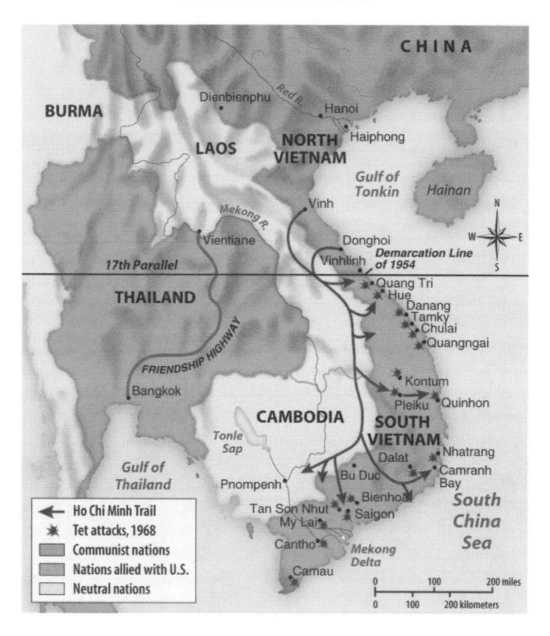

SFC Michael Di Rocco
US Army Special Forces (Ret.)

Special Forces Living with the Montagnards

De Oppresso Liber: To Liberate the Oppressed
U.S. Army Special Forces Motto

Mike Di Rocco's clandestine entry into Vietnam began on a moonless night in the Viet Cong-controlled Van Canh valley, 200 miles north of Saigon. The twelve-member Special Forces team's mission: organize, equip, train and lead a mercenary army of South Vietnam's indigenous tribesmen, the *Montagnards*.

Born in 1938 of Italian immigrants, Michael 'Mike' Di Rocco was highly trained in military engineering, explosives, and communications. He joined the Marines in 1954, serving as a tank commander and an Italian interpreter for NATO. In 1960, he joined the Army specifically for Special Forces. He served three tours of duty in Vietnam, 1962-1963; 1964, when he was badly wounded and returned to the U.S. to recover; and 1969, when he returned to Vietnam. He retired from the Army as a Sergeant First Class in 1973.

Special Forces History

The primary mission of the Army Special Forces is to train and lead unconventional warfare (UW) forces, or a clandestine guerrilla force in an occupied nation. Special Forces predecessors in unconventional warfare include American Revolution notable Francis Marion, aka the Swamp Fox; the U.S. 6th Army Special Reconnaissance Unit, aka the Alamo Scouts; and Wild Bill Donovan's OSS in WWII. In June 1952, the 10th Special Forces Group (Airborne) was formed under Col. Aaron Bank soon after the establishment of the Psychological Warfare School.

In 1961, to counter the expanding influence of Communist Viet Cong (VC) guerillas in South Vietnam, Special Forces "A" Teams, under a CIA umbrella (on loan from the Army), moved into small villages and hamlets of the Central Highlands. The teams were charged with developing civilian irregular defense groups (CIDG) from indigenous tribal populations such as the Montagnards.

Di Rocco at Jump School, 1960

Living with the Montagnards

The indigenous Montagnards (French, meaning *mountain dwellers* and pronounced *mon-ton-yards*), were recruited into service by the American Special Forces (aka the Green Berets) to defend their hamlets against the Viet Cong and serve as rapid response forces and intelligence gatherers. The mountain-dwelling Montagnards differed greatly from the lowland Vietnamese people in language, appearance, culture and religion, and were despised and seen as backward savages by North and South Vietnamese alike.

During their occupation, the French offered the country's indigenous populations protection and a high degree of autonomy. However, the Highland villagers were once again stripped of their rights in 1954 when the French were defeated by the Viet Minh Communists and withdrew from Vietnam.

Beginning in the 1960's, Special Forces twelve-member A-Teams were embedded in the Central Highlands villages, operating in remote areas and hostile environments with little external direction and support. The indigenous Montagnards, recruited into service by the American Special Forces, formed a special bond with the Green Berets. At the peak of the war there were more than two hundred teams and an army of more than 50,000 indigenous fighters who, like their trainers, were excellent warriors and used to a harsh environment.

Montagnard families often lived within the Special Forces encampments, refusing to leave their loved ones -- a further catalyst for the warriors' ferocity in battle. According to Di Rocco, "the Montagnards wanted nothing to do with South Vietnam. Their loyalty was to the Special Forces A-Teams. We delivered their babies, taught them how to fight, and led them in engagements against the Viet Cong – everything." The feelings of admiration and loyalty were mutual.

Di Rocco (left) with recon mountain commandos, 1963

Above: The Montagnards were fierce warriors, familiar with unconventional weapons such as the bow and arrow.

District security chief and Di Rocco with his soldiers after battle at Mom village. Mike is the tall soldier, 4th from the right.

Painting from a photo of Mike on patrol in the Van Canh Valley by military illustrator and painter Max Grace.

Green Berets' Ingenuity: A Midnight Requisition

As the Viet Cong forces became aware of American activity in tribal hamlets, Special Forces teams increased training and security patrols of their camp. To aid in this effort, Mike's unit requested a 105 howitzer, or "105." Their captain was told that all the howitzers had been given to the South Vietnamese and the unit would have to *purchase* one.

Furious at the prospect of buying back their own equipment, the team devised a daring plan to steal a 105. They recruited a friend who was employed by CIA Air America to help them with their caper. The pilot, a crew chief, and two Green Berets climbed into a Sikorsky H-34 helicopter with an external sling load of 5,000 pounds and flew up the coast to the ARVN (Army of the Republic of Viet Nam) base camp which was carelessly guarded.

"While the chopper hovered, our guys threw netting around the howitzer and handed boxes of shells and fuses to the crew chief. Two ARVN soldiers stepped out of their tent. When they realized what was happening, they ran towards the chopper, waving their arms and cursing as the 105 cleared the sandbag emplacement." As they flew north, the triumphant American soldiers threw a mock salute at the ARVN artillerymen.

Fate of the Montagnards

After U.S. forces withdrew from Vietnam, the Montagnards were left to face the brutal retaliation of the North Vietnamese Communist forces. The Communist government colonized their land, burned villages and killed thousands in a program of "ethnic cleansing." Those few who managed to escape Vietnam made their way through Cambodia and Laos to camps in Thailand, many of them perishing at the hands of the Khmer Rouge in Cambodia. Those who remain are still oppressed and despised. The Montagnard culture is on the verge of extinction.

After the war, the Americans who worked with the "Yards" in the Highlands, understanding the price they would pay, formed an organization to travel to Thailand to rescue Montagnards and bring them to America. Most of the Montagnards settled in North Carolina near Fort Bragg, home of their comrades, the Army's Special Forces.

In October 2019, North Carolina Senators Richard Burr and Thom Tillis introduced a resolution to recognize the contributions of the Montagnards, condemning ongoing human rights violations by the Socialist Republic of Vietnam.

Still Serving His Community

Mike Di Rocco is a self-described adventurer. While in Special Forces, he completed German mountain climbing school in Mittenwald and mountain and glacier climbing school in Aosta, Italy. He also led an expedition of Special Forces military and Italian underwater society divers to ancient Roman galleons, recovering artifacts for the Italian Bureau of Antiquities, Livorno, Italy. Mike and his wife Maggie live in Brevard, NC. He is currently on the Board of Directors of the Veterans History Museum of the Carolinas, serving in their mission to honor veterans, educate the community, and preserve important military artifacts.

Below: Mike Di Rocco, USMC 1954-1959
Right: Di Rocco, Special Forces 1960-1973

Mike wearing Green Beret jacket, 2019

Mike and Maggie Di Rocco, 2019

DAVID J. CRANDAL

USMC During the Early Vietnam War Years

From the military ID of David J. Crandal, age 20

In 1961, President Kennedy described the counterinsurgency in Vietnam as "another type of war, new in its intensity, ancient in its origin…. requiring a wholly different kind of military training." At that time, travelling from the Philippines to the Bay of Siam (now the Bay of Thailand), twenty-year old Marine Corporal David J. Crandal, like most Americans, had never heard of Vietnam.

Crandal enlisted in the Marines in 1959. After boot camp in San Diego, he completed infantry training at Camp Pendleton, then returned to San Diego for communications school. He was shipped to Okinawa and shortly thereafter to Japan's Mt. Fuji for cold weather training at the U.S. Marines Combined Arms Training Center, called Camp Fuji. "I'm not sure how long I was there, but it was long enough to know that I didn't like it."

Private Crandal prior to being shipped overseas

After returning to Okinawa, Crandal spent much of his time on daily military maneuvers as a member of the Artillery Battalion of the 3rd Marine Division, 12th Marines. At night, the Marines enjoyed "Cinderella Liberty," so-named because troops had to be back on base by midnight.

"One day, we returned from maneuvers at 3 p.m. and were told there would be no liberty that night. We were instructed to pack our field transport packs and put everything else into our sea bags, which we might never see again. There was an enormous amount of ammunition and artillery in numerous bunkers. We spent twenty-four hours a day for four days carrying heavy ammunition cases from the bunkers to ships." The Marines were flown to the Philippines and eventually Crandal found himself on a Marine helicopter carrier bound for the Bay of Siam.

Radio Communications on a Helo Carrier

During his service off the coast of Thailand, Crandal had two occupational specialties (MOS). Aboard the Marine Corps' only helicopter carrier, he trained Marines in radio communications, maps and coordinates. The primary task of the carrier was to take on damaged helicopters, replacing them with reconditioned choppers.

"One day I was on deck when an approaching helicopter dropped straight down into the water just as it reached the ship. Immediately, lots of little sampans rowed out from every direction to rescue the pilots. It looked like a wagon wheel with spokes. The pilots were saved, but they were shaken up. Many of the helicopters we received had been patched up in the field with duct tape. At this time, we were supposedly just 'advisors' in Vietnam; but people were being killed and these helicopters all had holes in them."

Artillery Forward Observer

Crandal's second MOS was as an Artillery Forward Observer for Communications with Naval Gunfire. To respond quickly to a situation, the military devised Battalion Landing Teams. The teams were comprised of specialists from different companies who were versed in radio communications, Morse code, artillery observation and spotting. The Navy called in these versatile teams as reinforcement when they needed to get things done quickly. As a Forward Observer, Crandal went ashore and directed the ship's gunners to specific targets, giving them the coordinates and then correcting fire after observing where the artillery hit. During his two years overseas, he served on eleven ships.

Crandal returned to San Francisco from Southeast Asia by ship in 1962. He did not encounter demonstrators, since most of the country was still unaware of any U.S. military action in Vietnam. However, his was not a joyous return. "We got off the ship and there was nobody there, except for a few parents. My parents were 3,000 miles away. It was not much of a homecoming. I appreciate that Vietnam veterans are now being acknowledged for their service during a tragic time in American history."

David and his wife, Penny, live in the Blue Ridge Mountains near Asheville, NC. David enjoys hiking and trail building and Penny, a Rotarian, participates in raising funds to eradicate polio and to aid in Alzheimer's research. The couple also enjoys keeping up with their eight children and seven "grands."

David Crandal in the Vietnam room at the Veterans History Museum of the Carolinas, 2019

David and Penny Colman Crandal

Andrew W. "Gunny" Boyko
Two Eras, Two Kinds of Warfare

LCpl Boyko manning his machine gun on a French bunker, 1965.

Andrew W. "Gunny" Boyko joined the Marines in 1964 and was sent to Vietnam in August 1965. During his two tours in Vietnam from 1965 to 1968, it seemed as if he were fighting in two different wars. During his first tour in Vietnam from 1965-1966, the enemy was a guerrilla organization that did not fight traditional battles. "When on patrol, the worst we encountered were ambushes, booby traps and sniper fire." By the time the Marines returned fire, the Viet Cong had vanished. "On the second tour, we dealt with the North Vietnamese Army (NVA). They did not give up; they did not surrender. It was a bloody fight every time we engaged."

First Tour: Guerilla Warfare Near Da Nang

"I joined the Marines in 1964. When I was in boot camp, I remember a drill instructor walking in with a newspaper saying, 'There's a conflict brewing in Vietnam. In a year we'll be over there fighting for our lives.' We looked at each other and said, 'What the hell is a Vietnam? I've never heard of it before.' I got there in August 1965. I wasn't on the first wave, but I was there at the beginning of the war."

In 1965 Boyko was assigned to help start an ammo dump (ASP-1) in the Da Nang area, near Hill 327 and later to Red Beach on a security detachment. As a Listening Post (LP), Boyko and another Marine acted as the early warning system for their company, going out in front of the lines after dark and reporting enemy movement. On one occasion, they went out so far, they received mortar fire from their own troops. "I buried my face in the sand and tried to crawl into my helmet and pull it up after me."

President Lyndon Johnson visiting Regional Landing Team 27th Marines on 2/17/68 as they prepare to embark for Vietnam. Boyko is second from the left.

When Boyko returned to the U.S. after thirteen months, he assumed his time in Vietnam was over.

Second Tour: Conventional Warfare

On the morning of January 31, 1968, North Vietnamese and Communist Viet Cong forces launched a coordinated attack against targets all over South Vietnam. The *Tet Offensive* greatly escalated American military involvement. Boyko was sent back to Vietnam with the 27th Marine Regimental landing team to help quell the invasion.

Demolition Man

While on patrol, if someone hit or found a booby trap or mine, everyone froze. Boyko, serving as a demolition man for the company, disarmed it or blew it up. It was exhausting work, yet as soon as he finished, the order 'Saddle up, we're moving out!' was passed. "I never got a break. I didn't even have time for a cigarette!" At night, the pain of shin splints kept Boyko awake. "I had very little sleep and was always exhausted."

Supplies were forever short. "I received explosives, a time fuse, and blasting caps, but no crimping tool. I learned to bite down on the hollow end of the blasting cap to crimp it onto the time fuse. Biting the wrong end of the cap would have caused it to explode in my face. The first explosives I received were quarter-pound blocks of TNT. Later I got C-4, which I loved. The C-4 also served as a heat tab to cook our C-rations. When lit with a match it produced enough heat to warm a meal without exploding."

Unlike other wars, the war in Vietnam was not a war to take territory. "The objective was to kill as many of the enemy as possible. We'd go up one hill and engage the enemy. After we'd taken the hill, usually with significant losses, we were told to proceed to a second hill. And then a third. Then they'd say to us, 'Remember that hill you took two weeks ago? Well, they're back, go take it again.' Most of us felt like bait. But as Marines we did what we were told to do."

Cpl Boyko at Red Beach, 1966.

"At one point, we set up in a schoolhouse south of Hue City near the Perfume River which did not smell *anything* like perfume! We knew that often when we smelled body odor, we were smelling ourselves. So, we tried to jump in the river to get cleaned off. Unfortunately, often snipers fired on us from the other side, so whenever we jumped in the water, we had one armed guy there to return fire while we bathed. That was normal."

In May 1968, the 27th Marines were part of Operation Allen Brook on Go Noi Island where their mission was to clear the island and the surrounding area of Viet Cong Communist forces and the North Vietnam Army. "The enemy forces were everywhere, and we needed help. At night, while in my quickly dug fighting hole, I saw a streak of red light come from the sky and heard a hum or a roar. Then it repeated. I thought, 'I've been in the field too long. I'm hallucinating. It's Martians invading and they're using ray guns.' Someone explained to me that it was one of our weapons called 'Puff the Magic Dragon.'" The Douglas AC-47 (nicknamed *Spooky* or *Puff the Magic Dragon*) was a fixed-wing gunship designed to provide heavy firepower when ground forces needed close air support. "They were using a Gatling gun that fired 6,000 rounds a minute, which is why it sounded like a roar or hum rather than staccato machine gun fire. I was really glad they were on our side that night."

Coming Home

Returning to the U.S. was a horror Boyko could not comprehend. "I had to learn quickly not to let anybody know I was a combat veteran. We were called baby and women killers. It was so painful because I was proud that I'd served my country." When Boyko got out of the Marines in 1968, he thought he was done with them forever.

Seven years later, because of his combat experience, Boyko was asked to return to the Marine Corps in the Reserves to help form a reconnaissance unit in Encino, CA. He accepted the challenge and enjoyed serving his country again. He was assigned to S-2 as a Scout Radio Operator with the 2nd Battalion 23rd Marine regiment. Later, he transferred to El Toro to become an Armorer for the base. When the helicopters came to get their 50 cal machine guns, Boyko went with them as part of the crew.

Today, Boyko works as a volunteer with the Transylvania County Sheriff's Office, transporting prisoners and assisting as firearms range officer. He served as President of the Fleet Reserve Association, Commander of the American Legion, officer in the Marine Corps League, VFW and the DAV. He is the chairman of the Brevard, NC Memorial Day parade and ceremony.

Andy and his wife Trudy live on the crest of a hill overlooking the French Broad River and North Carolina farmlands -- a far cry from Hill 327 and Hue City in South Vietnam.

2019: Andy Boyko at the Marine Corps 50th anniversary reunion, Washington D.C.

Andy Boyko

Poem written by Andy Boyko, based on an actual incident on December 23, 1965

The Night Before Christmas

Christmas Eve night in a foxhole for two
I stared at the night, with nothing to do.
When all of a sudden, there came such a clatter
I raised for my rifle, to see what's the matter.

I looked at the dark, past the barbed wire
My heart was pounding, my brain was on fire
It's an enemy probe or a full-blown charge.
Got to act now, no time to call Sarge!

Footsteps I hear, in my garden of death,
I hold my rifle, and even my breath.
But what if he's friendly and got lost in the night?
I'll yell out a challenge and conceal my fright.

He keeps coming at me, won't even break stride.
My God, I'm scared, there's no place to hide!
I raise up my rifle and squeeze on my gun.
Visions of horror are not too much fun.

I pull on the trigger, it jumps in my hand,
I spray my bullets on this god-awful land.
Silence now, all is quite still.
How many men tonight did kill?

A hero I'll be with the coming of dawn
When they count up the bodies on my barbed-wire lawn.
When morning came, I felt real fine.
When Sarge came out to check on my line.

He roared and he laughed with his hands on his belly.
To him it was funny, but my knees turned to jelly.
"It's not the enemy you happened to kill."
A water buffalo lay at the base of the hill.

Now you may laugh, but I tell you no lie.
The line I held … and no one got by.
While back in the States folks were snug in their beds
With visions of Christmas dancing 'round in their heads,
I'd stayed in my foxhole, concealed my fright.
MERRY CHRISTMAS, YOU GUYS, 'TWAS A HELL OF A NIGHT!

Welcome Home, Brother

JAMES CLARK MURRAY
Big Guns on the Ho Chi Minh Trail

Clark Murray, Texas A&M, 1967

Fort Lauderdale High School senior James "Clark" Murray never imagined that his proficiency in mathematics would lead him to a remote jungle village in South Vietnam, close to the Cambodian border.

The son of a WWII anti-aircraft artillery officer, Murray entered Texas A&M University on an ROTC scholarship. "At that time, A&M was more like a military academy. The school had been the leading provider of officers in WWII. Students that attended A&M had a head start when they joined the military. I had a good math background, which is one reason the artillery appealed to me."

Cold War Defense

After receiving his commission in 1967 and attending artillery school at Fort Sill, Oklahoma, Murray was assigned to an M107 self-propelled 175mm artillery division near

Frankfurt, Germany. "The cold war was hot then. Most of our weapons with corps artillery were 175's, the big guns that could shoot a round fifteen to eighteen miles. Our army was positioned there to prevent Russia from coming through to Germany."

Murray was given a battery as a First Lieutenant. "This is a captain's or major's job. But all the captains and majors were in Vietnam. They promoted these young guys who didn't know much about leadership. I was fortunate because of my experience at A&M, which was vitally important. I learned a lot about leadership in the year I was stationed in Germany."

The Tet Offensive and a New Form of Army War

During the early hours of January 31, 1968, during the Vietnamese lunar new year (or "Tet") holiday, North Vietnam and Viet Cong forces staged simultaneous attacks against five major South Vietnamese cities, dozens of military installations, and scores of towns and villages throughout South Vietnam. The U.S. and South Vietnamese militaries sustained heavy losses. "There was a critical need in Vietnam, so I volunteered. I felt that Vietnam was where I needed to be after all my training."

Lightweight 105 Horwitzer

Murray returned from Germany to the states to marry his sweetheart, Bunny, and 28 days later they were in Seattle preparing for deployment. A week of jungle training in the snow and ice was followed by the newlyweds' tearful separation.

On December 12, 1968, Murray reported for command to the 5th Battalion, 22nd Artillery in Pleiku, in the high-altitude region of South Vietnam's Central Highlands. "You can't believe the destruction there. Everything was bombed out, and we were trying to organize to move forward." Three days later, he was promoted to Captain and assigned to B Battery, 22nd Artillery Provisional at Ban Me Thout Airbase in charge of a composite battery of 105mm and 155mm howitzers.

Located at a little place called Duc Lap in the jungle about three miles from the Cambodian border, the battery's mission was to defend the Duc Lap Special Forces camp. Besides U.S. Special Forces and Murray's artillery battery, the camp included ARVN (Army of the Republic of Vietnam) forces. There were no U.S. troops. The location was of critical importance because of its proximity to the Ho Chi Minh Trail, a major enemy infiltration route on which North Vietnamese carried essential supplies to the Viet Cong in South Vietnam. Duc Lap was the first major area of resistance to the NVA as they came into South Vietnam from Cambodia. As such, it was under constant attack. "It was a god-awful place. Terrible temperatures. Constant rain during the monsoon season and summers so hot and dusty that we could hardly breathe.

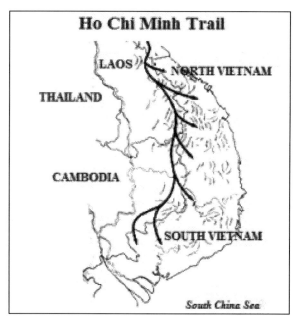

The Ho Chi Minh Trail

"The Army's war in Vietnam was not like other Army wars. Normally, the Army is on the move, taking territory. In Vietnam we sat on our hill and waited for the enemy to come to us. Every camp had a perimeter that had to be defended. That's why the composite batteries were so successful. We were able to provide supporting fire so that fire bases were not overrun.

"The camps were designed so that we never kept all our artillery pieces in one place. We didn't have any air support, so we put artillery pieces for defensive fires in a split camp -- 105's on one hill and 155's on another, about 4 klicks away. This way we provided strong firepower but reduced the risk of losing all artillery pieces at one time.

"You can't lead with a radio." Murray often travelled between two camps through enemy territory.

"I was extremely vulnerable as I travelled by Jeep between the camps, through enemy territory. You can't lead with a radio – you must be with your men. I had capable officers, but they needed guidance. Many of them had no military background except a little bit of ROTC. In Duc Lap, every assignment I had was larger than I felt ready for, but I just had to rise to the occasion. I kept driving forward, not sitting around thinking, 'This is crazy, what am I doing here?'

"My first sergeant, Top, was invaluable to me. My job included more than the military aspect of war. There were administrative and operations tasks as well. Top was schooled in those areas as a non-com. And when it came to personnel matters, decisions that involved tough choices, I'd ask, 'What would you do, Top?' I was just twenty-one and he was older. He really helped me gain self-confidence and taught me to take the initiative."

Hazards Defending the Perimeter

Artillery defense of the Duc Lap camp perimeters required mathematical proficiency. Accurate fire was essential. "We had to set our guns so that they were as close to the perimeter as possible because the enemy was very good at getting close. They knew they were safer near the perimeter because we didn't want to shoot our own people. We always had this terrible decision. If somebody makes a mistake, then our guys are dead. That's what gave me the most nightmares and chills – the fear of making a mistake that killed our guys. Praise God, that never happened on my watch, but it happened on many others. Not necessarily because they weren't good soldiers, but it was usually a moving situation and if you didn't have good intelligence and feedback, it was easy to make an error that you'd regret for the rest of your life."

Jungle Warfare

Besides perimeter defense, B Battery provided support for Special Forces and ARVN troops in the jungle. "We were on the Ho Chi Minh Trail, so the infiltration was right down past us. Special Forces and ARVN were working the border trying to flush out the enemy and interrupt their supply flow. When trouble broke out, we would wait on our fire missions, based on their command from the ground. Usually, when all hell broke loose, they would have small arms fire for about twenty minutes and then they would get the heck out of there and call in the artillery."

"The trail was seldom visible. The overgrowth in the jungle was so massive that we couldn't see the sky in many places. When you're trying to direct artillery fire, you need to know where the round hit, and you don't want to hit your own man. We would set a proximity fuse so that the bomb would detonate above the canopy, and then our spotter would adjust our fire according to instructions from the guy on the ground. Every fire mission we prayed, 'Oh, God, I hope we get this right.'"

Life in Camp

Murray described the challenges of everyday life in the artillery camp. "The weather was the most significant factor in our ordeal. We lived on a 3,000-foot hill made from clay, dust, mud, and dirt. We dug trenches and put big covers over them to protect ourselves from the rain and the enemy. The worst time I've ever had was during the monsoon season. There were always at least twelve inches of water and mud in the bunkers, and we'd slog around in our holes. Often our feet got stuck in the mud. We hung our hammocks from the rafters.

"And the rats! There were so many rats in my hooch that I slept with a .45 in my hand. I'd feel a rat moving across my chest and I'd shoot it – it took about four or five rounds to figure out where the little guy was. It was the ugliest feeling to be in a deep, exhausted sleep and then feel a rat on my face. The shooting occurred in the enlisted quarters, too. It was crazy stuff."

Murray devised an elaborate shower system for the troops which offered much appreciated fresh water. They elevated 55-gallon drums and pumped water from the periodic tankers that came to the compound. "We would sit in grime and filth for a week or more, so it was wonderful to have fresh water that we could actually swallow. To this day, I can feel that fresh, lukewarm water coming down."

Although Murray's battery endured constant assaults, they were never overrun. He attributes this not only to his men but to the invaluable support of the area's brave Montagnards. "They lived with their families in our camp and the men fought fiercely to protect their loved ones. They stuck to it and were very loyal to the Americans. Without them, we would have lost many more men."

Helicopter dropping supplies at Duc Lap Camp landing zone

Liberty and Loss

After ten months in Vietnam, Murray returned to Hawaii for R&R, meeting his wife Bunny for a much-anticipated honeymoon. While he was there, three of his best soldiers were killed. The men had been in the Fire Detection Center – a bunker that had small viewing slots. Unfortunately, the North Vietnamese were skilled at positioning their RPG's into the slot. One of the rounds entered and killed all three men, including Top -- Murray's advisor, friend and battery sergeant. "Top had four kids. It was so sad and I knew if I'd been there, I probably would have been in that bunker. I still think about that and wonder 'Why not me, Lord?'"

Returning to Vietnam, Murray was assigned to an ARVN compound where he directed massive amounts of artillery and air power. It was another learn-as-you-go situation for him. "One time the enemy got into the wire and the trenches. It was frightening because I didn't know what was going on; I just had to continue my mission and trust that somebody had my back. On another occasion, when military brass were visiting, the enemy fired 122mm rockets into the compound, killing four officers about ten meters from my bunker. My ears are still ringing from that explosion."

Seattle and the Wall

In October 1969, Murray left Vietnam, flying into Seattle, his drop point. "There was an unbelievable protest in the airport terminal. It was a shock because we'd heard other people talk about what was going on back home, but we didn't understand the magnitude of the protests. When I got off the plane, I was spat on many times. Some of the troops wanted to fight; they blew up. I felt so sorry for the soldiers. These guys lived in hell for so long. They were afraid for their lives every hour of the day. Then they came home to derision from so many. It was a small part of America, but it was heartbreaking for our troops. We weren't prepared for what we encountered. It was terrible."

Many years later, Murray visited the Wall in Washington, D.C. "I cried like a baby. I went and found my cadre of folks who had died, including my friends and classmates from A&M; but my first sergeant, Top, was the one on my heart and mind. I cried the whole time I was near the Wall."

We Will Always Remember

"My mission was to create an environment that was as secure as possible for those troopers under my command, and to give them a sense that their leader was 100% behind them and respected them. Respect and loyalty are so important, especially in a time of war when you're dealing with men's lives.

"In Vietnam, I served with some of the best people I've ever known in my career. They were of high character and quality. I was so blessed by them. I think that in a combat situation, you gravitate to the good in things because that's all you have.

"I'll always remember those young men and women and their talents, dedication, and loyalty. We weren't respected when we came home. But on the other side of the coin, we remember the camaraderie and the love of our country, and the great men that we served with. They can't take that away from us."

Clark Murray in Washington, DC, on a Blue Ridge Honor Flight, 2018.

Clark and Meredith "Bunny" Murray

MCPO Clyde Jones, USN (Ret.)
The Big E: A Recipe for Success

CPO Clyde Jones, Orlando, 1974

It's been said that an Army marches on its stomach, attesting to the importance of well-provisioned forces in the military. For Clyde Jones, *serving* in the Navy took on new meaning as he directed the preparation of 15,000 meals a day for the hungry Sailors, Marines and Air Wing 9 aboard USS Enterprise, nicknamed the "Big E."

The son of Winfred and Martha Jones, Clyde and his eight siblings grew up on a 120-acre farm in Lake Toxaway, NC, where everything was accomplished by hand, horses, and mules. Five of the seven brothers served in the U.S. military. Clyde enlisted in 1954 at age 18, retiring 32 years later as a Master Chief Petty Officer, the highest non-commissioned rank in the U.S. Navy.

Life Aboard the Big E

In 1965, the Navy was looking for volunteers to serve aboard USS *Enterprise*, the world's first nuclear powered aircraft carrier. The carrier's power plant consisted of eight nuclear reactors, four sets of turbines and four shafts. Petty Officer First Class Jones volunteered. "My Leading Chief sat me down and said, 'Jones, you've had eight years in the Navy, but you've never been on a ship like this. You've got to be top notch. Everyone must conform to the high *Enterprise* standards.'"

Enterprise was deployed in 1965 for service in Vietnam and became the first nuclear-powered ship to engage in combat when she launched bomb-laden aircraft executing 125 sorties against the Viet Cong near Bien Hoa City. The next day, she launched a record-breaking 165 strike sorties in a single day.

CVN-65, nicknamed Big E, was the first carrier of its kind, powered solely by its eight nuclear reactors.

A leader in the ship's company, Jones oversaw S-2 Division, a section of the Supply Department. "My job was feeding 5,000 troops – that's 15,000 meals a day. Energy levels had to be replenished on a constant basis. The mess hall was open 22 hours a day in order to feed troops around the clock." Supervising 75 professional cooks and bakers and numerous mess attendants was only part of Jones' busy routine. He was also responsible for requisitioning, receipt, stowage and issuance of all foodstuffs used in the general mess. Cleaning and maintenance of seven mess decks, six storerooms, three "reefer banks" and all food and vegetable preparation areas required the concerted efforts of all the members of the division.

Cooks, bakers and attendants worked around the clock, preparing 15,000 meals a day.

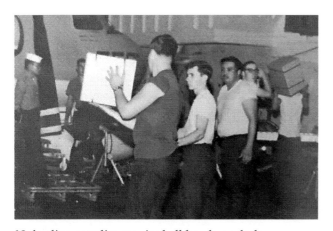

Unloading supplies required all hands on deck.

Helicopters transferred provisions to the ship's flight deck, elevators carried the supplies to the hangar bay, and items were manhandled down into the lower storerooms, hand-over-hand. "It took all-hands-on-deck, from the lowest seaman to the commanding officer, to get the job done. It required a lot of coordination, but we were a well-oiled team."

Breakfast and Bombs

Meals were available around the clock, depending on the schedules of the ship's personnel. "Everyone learned early on when to hit the chow line." The forward mess hall was the *speed line* – hamburgers, hot dogs, fried chicken in 30 minutes. The after gallery provided larger, more complicated meals. "We practiced progressive cooking all along the line. To feed 5,000 people breakfast, you prepare 100 portions at a time, like in a restaurant."

Besides accommodating hungry sailors, the forward mess hall also housed bombs from the lower decks where the ordnance men (*red shirts*) prepared them for transfer to the flight deck and waiting aircraft. Personnel complacently munched French fries and hot dogs next to the ordnance -- fast food and bomb assembly.

Sailors dine, used to ordnance stored in the forward mess hall on its way to the flight deck.

The USS *Enterprise* was the pride and joy of Admiral Hyman G. Rickover, the father of nuclear power. "We used to call him the daddy of the *Enterprise*. He'd sneak on board. He was hell on security. In 53 years, the *Enterprise* never had a problem with security." Dignitaries often toured the Big E, including Hollywood stars. "Martha Raye was with us. We also had excellent country music bands."

Clyde is extremely proud of the Big E and his time on board. "I have to brag a bit on the *Enterprise*. She served in the Atlantic and Pacific fleets for 53 years, during the Cuban missile crisis and many tours in Vietnam and the Middle East. She has always performed above and beyond."

During Clyde's first tour, all personnel attached to the aircraft carrier received the Navy Commendation Medal for outstanding heroism in action against the enemy. The award is the second highest given for an entire ship. The citation reads: *"In all operations, the Enterprise's performance was distinguished by professional and exacting thoroughness....The courage, perseverance and dedication displayed by the officers and men of the Enterprise and Attack Carrier Wing 9 were in keeping with the tradition of the United States Naval Service."*

Brown Water Navy: Serving on a Swift Boat Support Vessel

After two-and-a-half tours on the Big E, Clyde, now a Chief Petty Officer, attended Naval Amphibious Counterinsurgency School in Jacksonville, FL, and returned to Vietnam in support duty for small river craft that had been hit by the Viet Cong. "I was on the USS *Tutuila*, known as the mother-hen. We stayed tied up and the small craft would come along side of us. We'd lift them up on the dry dock and repair them there."

Once a month, Jones travelled by truck to Long Binh for provisions. "We carried our supplies in enclosed vehicles. Anything that wasn't padlocked would be stolen by the locals who rode alongside the truck on mopeds and lifted the supplies."

Patrol boats provided security for the mother-hen 24/7. In order to thwart sapper attacks (explosives attached to the ship by VC swimmers), gunners' mates continually lobbed grenades into the water. "It was no picnic. I was glad to go home."

USS Tutuila taking on a riverboat for repairs

Stateside Again

Clyde's return to the United States mirrors that of many Vietnam veterans. In both Alameda, CA, and Jacksonville, FL, Clyde and his shipmates were treated badly. "It got very nasty. We were instructed to keep our composure and avoid trouble. It was especially hard for the younger guys, the combat troops. So many of their buddies died over there and when they returned, they were called baby killers. Some of them still can't deal with it."

Clyde was made Master Chief Petty Officer in 1981. His last duty station was at the Naval Air Station in Pensacola where he managed the BEQ (Bachelor Enlisted Quarters). His Navy evaluation reported: *His exceptional technical competence and supervisory ability are clearly evident in the outstanding results he achieved in all assigned tasks.*

Clyde married Evelyn Dishman in November 1973. (She died in a car accident in 2005.) After Clyde retired in 1986, the couple purchased a home in Brevard, NC, where he worked for the City of Brevard in the Water Department, reading water meters for ten years. "I loved the walking. It kept me in good shape."

Master Chief Petty Officer Jones

Reunion

The USS *Enterprise's* last mission was a week-long inactivation ceremony in 2012 which included a reunion and memorial service at Naval Station Norfolk. All USS *Enterprise* veterans, their families, shipyard workers, and friends of the Big E were invited to attend, and thousands of veterans appeared to say goodbye. Clyde Jones, of course, was in attendance. "It was a four-day reunion, and everyone came to honor the Big E, including admirals, retired admirals, captains, generals, and the Chief of Naval Operations. Every commanding officer since 1961 still living attended. At dinner, ninety-three-year-old Admiral Holloway, who served as Chief of Naval Operations from 1974–1978, spoke to us via video. He told us, 'Sorry I can't be there guys. My wife won't let me fly any more, but congratulations and carry on as usual.' When we went aboard, they told us, 'Leave your hat. There won't be any saluting on the hangar bay because if there were, you wouldn't be doing anything *but* saluting.'"

Final Words

"I am proud to have served 32 years in the greatest military service in the world, the United States Navy. And I'm proud to have been able to serve the greatest country in the world. God Bless the United States of America."

On Jones' third tour aboard the USS *Enterprise,* the entire crew and her embarked air wing received the Navy Unit Commendation Ribbon.

THE SECRETARY OF THE NAVY
WASHINGTON

The Secretary of the Navy takes pleasure in commending

USS ENTERPRISE (CVA(N)-65)
AND
ATTACK CARRIER AIR WING NINE

for service as set forth in the following

CITATION:

For exceptionally meritorious service from 18 December 1966 to 20 June 1967 while serving as a unit of the U. S. SEVENTH Fleet during combat operations against enemy aggressor forces in North Vietnam. During this period, USS ENTERPRISE and her embarked air wing carried out day and night aerial strikes for 132 days in an environment of intense enemy antiaircraft fire and surface-to-air missiles. Employing all-weather capable strike aircraft, special detection device-equipped aircraft and all other assets, ENTERPRISE units aggressively pursued systematic and highly effective attacks against logistic-type targets, thermal power plants, airfields, major storage areas, steel plants, and surface-to-air missile sites in North Vietnam. In all operations, ENTERPRISE's performance was distinguished by professional and exacting thoroughness, skillful planning and execution, and intelligent application of naval air striking power, resulting in the infliction of extensive and severe damage to the enemy. The courage, stamina, perseverance, and dedication displayed by the officers and men of ENTERPRISE and embarked Attack Carrier Air Wing NINE were in keeping with the highest traditions of the United States Naval Service.

All personnel attached to USS ENTERPRISE, or to her embarked air wing, and serving on board this vessel during the period designated above, or any part thereof, are hereby authorized to wear the Navy Unit Commendation Ribbon.

Paul R. Ignatius
Secretary of the Navy

JONES, CLYDE C. 967 53 51

FINISH FILE PERS E3ra

In a 1951 movie, Jerry Lewis sang "the Navy gets the gravy, but the Army gets the beans" which holds true in the February 5, 1968 offering in the mess hall aboard the Big E.

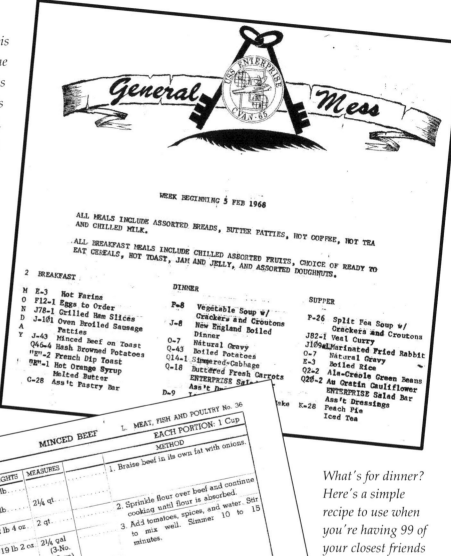

What's for dinner? Here's a simple recipe to use when you're having 99 of your closest friends to dinner.

Sgt. Howard A. Thiele, USA (Ret.)
Vietnam from the Driver's Seat

Howard Thiele at base camp with M-14

Eighteen-year-old Army recruit Howard A. "Sarge" Thiele was one of 3,800 troops who left California for Vietnam on the USS *William S. Weigle* in September 1966. The 30-day trip with several stops included a memorable 12 hours in Okinawa, where Thiele and his good friend Hugo "Butch" Miele spent hours in a bar, staggering back to the ship just in time. Little did Thiele know that years later Butch would be instrumental in getting him out of Vietnam alive.

Nervous Landing

After stopping at several ports along the coast of Vietnam, the troop ship arrived at Qui Nhon, a coastal city in central Vietnam. "There was no pier in Qui Nhon, so we went over the side of the ship with rope ladders, like in WWII. They put us on landing craft to take us ashore. We didn't know what to expect. We were just scared to death."

The nervous new recruits loaded their weapons and camouflaged their faces with cigar ashes. "The landing craft pulled up to the beach where people were in bathing suits, drinking Cokes. We felt like the world's biggest bunch of idiots. They loaded us in buses and took us to our base camp, Camp Addison, in the Cha Rang Valley on Highway 19.

Eighth Transportation Group

Thiele was a heavy truck driver with the 523rd Transportation Company. Truck transport was the most cost-effective and available means of carrying supplies throughout Vietnam to support U.S. troops. The 8th Transportation Group ferried supplies from the coastal ports of Qui Nhon and Cam Ranh Bay to inland bases, hauling anything from socks and uniforms to bombs, ammunition and food supplies. "We called it beans and bullets."

Howard "Sarge" Thiele at base camp

The road travel was extremely hazardous. "The concept of winning a war is to stop the enemy from being supplied. The U.S. mission was to stop supplies coming down the Ho Chi Minh Trail, and the Viet Cong and NVA had the same mission – to stop supplies from reaching our troops."

During his first tour, Thiele drove five-ton cargo trucks throughout the Central Highlands, especially along Highway 19. For the first few months, the drivers' biggest challenges were weather and road conditions. "It was the monsoon season with torrential rain and temperatures up to 118 degrees. It was hot, miserable and dusty. The unpaved roads were full of potholes and mortar holes. Our heavy trucks had to climb two steep passes – the An Khe Pass and the Mang Yang Pass -- with many switchback turns. Maximum speed with foot-on-the-floorboard was eight-to-ten miles an hour.

"This was all on Highway 19. The faster trucks literally pushed the slower trucks up the mountain, bumper-to-bumper. The 90-mile trip took ten or twelve hours. Often when we got there, we slept in our trucks and returned the next day. The maintenance on the trucks was our biggest problem. There wasn't a single day when we didn't have one, two, or sometimes three flat tires to repair when we got back to base camp. It was a lot of hard work."

Soon these predictable routes with difficult driving conditions and slow-moving vehicles became targets for enemy ambushes. The winding, steep mountain road,

Truck demolished truck on Ambush Alley

bordered by fields and woods, was dubbed *Ambush Alley*. "They had several ways of ambushing us, such as mines, satchel charges, RPGs, and small arms fire. There were brush and trees within five or ten yards of the road, enabling them to hide easily. They enemy was so close to the road that it was hard to miss us. By sheer volume of fire, they were able to kill a lot of Americans. We had one Jeep with an

M-60 machine gun and the rest of our weapons were semi-automatic. At that time, the M-14 was all we had, and it was a matter of 'how fast can you pull the trigger?' It was very cumbersome."

Ammo Dump Explosion

Convoys on An Khe Pass were were easy, predictable targets.

On one occasion, Thiele's convoy had to spend a night at LZ (landing zone) English, between Phu Cat Air Base and Bong Son on Highway 1 North, after delivering a load of bombs to the airstrip. The bombs were stored in a massive ammo dump. That night, the Viet Cong shelled the camp, igniting hundreds of tons of bombs in the ammunition dump. "We'd been sleeping in our trucks, but we jumped out and hit the dirt. A lot of our trucks had shrapnel and holes from the explosives. It was really scary, but only two of us were wounded and nobody was killed."

Gun Trucks Join the Convoys

As the ambushes intensified, the transport units began to provide their own immediate security. At first they accomplished this with armed jeeps, but these rapidly proved inadequate, so the Transportation Corps developed a new type of security vehicle which became known as the gun truck. "They started with M-60 machine guns mounted on pedestals. Then they got some 50-caliber machine guns and ultimately mini-guns which were 7.62mm Gatling guns, firing about 6,000 rounds a minute. They could put at least one round in every square foot of a football-field-sized target. The downside was that the gun trucks became the primary targets in ambushes.

Sarge on top of his 5-ton 6x6 Zorba

"Occasionally, several gun trucks accompanied us since some convoys were 100 trucks or more, stretching out for miles. During my second tour, I built the first gun truck for the 2nd Transportation Company in Phu Tai. I put armored plates across the sides, back, doors, and the windshield of a five-ton M-54 truck. The design was limited only by the builder's imagination and all gun trucks had different names. I named ours *Guns A-Go-Go*."

Friendly Hitchhikers

One unique load proved particularly rewarding. After dropping off his trailer in An Khe, Thiele was proceeding to his base camp when he spotted a group of men in uniform on the side of the road. "As I slowed, I realized they were American Marines, waving at me. I stopped and the gunny sergeant asked whether they could catch a ride with me. I was in the tractor, without my trailer. I told him that I had room in the cab for two people. He said, 'We'll hang on.'

"The Marines were standing on the running boards, on the fenders, up front and on the bedplates behind the cab. There were ten of us in that truck. They'd been part of a long-range patrol and they needed a ride back. They were real grunts. I took them about 35 miles that they would have had to walk. I felt like a million dollars after helping those guys. And I was the safest guy on the road. I was accompanied by the United States Marine Corps."

Purple Heart and Home

Sgt. Howard Thiele's first tour ended in October 1967. Returning to Vietnam for his second tour in January 1968, this time with 2nd Transportation Company in Phu Tai, he was surprised and pleased to greet his long-time friend Butch Miele in the same company.

Thiele was seriously wounded on August 12, 1968, while driving an 18-wheeler. "We were travelling between the passes on a hot, nasty day when we came upon a bridge they'd blown up. We were hauling extremely heavy loads of ammo and had to go down off the road, through a river and up the other side. Several vehicles got stuck and the Viet Cong command-detonated their mines.

"I ran over an anti-tank mine. The tractor only weighed about 12,000 pounds, so it was OK, but the trailer, loaded with bombs, weighed 70,000 pounds, which set off the anti-tank mine. The explosion went right up through the floorboards. I was wounded in a very uncomfortable spot and I couldn't sit down for a long time. We lost eight men and twelve were wounded. Twenty-six trucks out of the 40-truck convoy were destroyed, but we had to leave all 40 behind."

Hugo "Butch" Miele, Thiele's friend and mentor who had introduced him to Okinawa barhopping, pulled Thiele from his truck, supporting him and half-dragging him as they ran to rescuing helicopters from the 1st Cavalry Division in An Khe. "That was the last ambush I ever experienced."

Stateside

Upon his return to the states, Sarge married and had three children. He continued in transportation for eight years and eventually found his way into Air Defense. But the Army discovered that he was mechanically inclined and made him a motor sergeant. "I worked on track vehicles, APC's, missile launch stations, trucks, and Jeeps."

Thiele retired in 1987 and moved back to Florida, where he worked at Albertsons Grocery Stores from a bagboy to manager of one of the chain's liquor stores. He met and married Lori Swank fifteen years ago. "When I met her, my life changed. She's calmed me down quite a bit. She turned my life around."

Visiting the Wall

"I went to the wall in 1984. There's a kiosk where you give them the names of your loved ones or friends, and they tell you where they are on the wall. They had a dot-matrix printer which was very loud. I'll never forget this. I gave the names of three friends to the girl behind the counter. As I stood waiting, the printer started making the familiar *gggt-gggt-gggt* sound those printers used to create. When that happened, I just lost it right there. The girl behind the counter gave me a big hug. I'm glad I went, but I'll never go back. People say the wall gives you closure, but there's no closure for me. I'll never get those experiences out of my life."

Sarge and Lori moved to WNC in 2009. Lori works in her garden and delights in mountain snowstorms. Sarge stays busy as Commander of the Transylvania County Honor Guard.

Finding buddies on the wall.

"Who, me?" Sarge at an Honor Guard function.

Capt. Wendell "Ray" Alcorn, USN (Ret.)
Seven Years a Prisoner of War

Patch of Attack Squadron 36, nicknamed the Roadrunners

Captain Ray Alcorn's account, in his own words.

My brother, sister, and I grew up in a rural community near Snyderville, Pennsylvania, located in the western part of the state. I remember well the many evenings that I would lie in our back yard, watching the crossing contrails of the fighter aircraft practicing their tactics overhead. One day, as my brother and I were in a field baling hay, the National Guard were practicing their maneuvers in F102s overhead. A pilot came down low and passed over us at about 50 feet, then rolled up into the air. I told my brother, "Someday I'm going to trade in this tractor for one of those."

I graduated from Penn State University in 1961. My life-long dream of flying was finally realized in October when the U.S. Navy accepted me into their flight training program. On March 16, 1962, I proudly accepted my commission and began flight training. In June 1963, I became a qualified Naval Aviator. After a short tour at the Naval

Justice School, I arrived at Cecil Field, Florida, where I joined my squadron, Attack Squadron 36, flying the A4 Skyhawk.

Shortly after returning from a Mediterranean cruise aboard the USS *Saratoga*, my squadron joined Air Group 9 aboard the USS *Enterprise*, our country's first nuclear powered aircraft carrier and the largest and most powerful warship in our fleet.

LTjg Ray Alcorn prior to shootdown

Shoot-Down

We started flying missions in Vietnam on December 2, 1965. My first combat tour was cut short on December 22nd when, after 20 days and 29 combat missions, I was shot down and captured in North Vietnam.

On that day, we were to fly our first alpha strike, 90 airplanes going against a huge power plant complex outside the city of Hai Phong. The weather was terrible, about 400 foot overcast, 2-mile visibility and our Admiral sent word to Washington that we shouldn't fly this mission. Washington said, "Go hit it today. We don't care what you have to do."

We went in at 50 feet under the overcast -- the visibility so bad that we had to fly close together. We couldn't come in in opposing directions. We had flights of four in tight formation and we all dropped when the leader dropped. Ours was the third flight through. Just as I was dropping my bombs, I was hit in the cockpit, a shell went through my oxygen mask, another shell hit me in the side of the neck and the oxygen mask blew up. I was temporarily blinded.

At 500 miles per hour at 50 feet and unable to see, I had to make a quick decision. I'll always live with the question of whether I made the right decision, because in a matter of seconds I could see again. But by that time, I had ejected and was standing on the ground. I had lost the antenna off the top of my radio, therefore losing contact with my fellow pilots. Thus, I was reported as missing in action and for at least four years, nobody knew for sure whether I was alive.

Shootdown photo used by North Vietnamese for propaganda.

Up to my knees in the mud and water of a rice paddy, I went up over a dike and hid in a clump of trees in a ditch, covering myself with dirt and leaves. I could see 200 or so Vietnamese peasants coming across the field. They found me and pulled me out of the ditch. They were the North Vietnamese civil guard, a civilian contingent of their military. They carried WWI vintage rifles, pitchforks, sticks, clubs – whatever they could find to use as a weapon. Two guys held my arms and others tried to get my flight gear off. Navy flight gear is all zippers, and they had no idea how to operate a zipper.

An old guy cut my torso harness and removed most of my clothes. They brought over a kid and handed him a rifle with a fixed bayonet on it. The old guy with the knife cut my flight suit down the front and, pulling it back, pointed at my chest. And I'm thinking, 'Man, this is a bad way to go.' A guy with a camera took our picture. I saw it years later in a Vietnamese newspaper. A prison guard told me the caption said *"12-Year-Old Captures Yankee Air Pirate."*

No Geneva Convention

The people who captured me didn't harm me. Eventually they turned me over to the regular army, and the whole ambience changed. The soldiers tied me up, tightly blindfolded me, and put me in a jeep. We stopped before dark at a little medical shack where a guy in a dirty white smock pronounced that I was alright. I had some serious burns on my face, and my neck was bleeding quite a bit from the bullet wound. But he didn't do anything for me. Three armed guards took me back outside. A mob of 50 or 100 descended on us with stones, sticks, and clubs.

One of the things that helped me the most amid this melee was a little old Vietnamese woman, wrinkled and grey-haired, who reached out and put a small cake in my hand. **Then she stepped back and made the sign of the cross.**

By that time, it was dark. They put me in the middle of a path with a bunch of kerosene lights. A man who spoke English with a thick French accent asked me, "What is your name, rank, service number, and date of birth?" which is the only information you're allowed to give should you become a prisoner of war. Then he said, "Your code of conduct doesn't mean anything here. As far as we're concerned, you're among the blackest criminals in North Vietnam and that's how you're going to be treated."

Then he started asking me other questions which I refused to answer. I was sitting in a ring of lights and I couldn't see anybody around me. People would step in and hit me with a rifle butt or fists. They beat me up pretty bad. Frenchie finally said, "If you're not going to answer questions, we have no reason to keep you around." They dragged me over to a ditch, had me kneel, and put a gun to the back of my head. He said, "You have to the count of ten to answer our questions." He started counting. At ten somebody behind me fired a gun. That ended my first interrogation session.

Hanoi Hilton

I finally arrived at the *Hanoi Hilton* that night, a prison built by the French. Its real name was Hoa Lo, which means Hell's Hole. They put me in a little section of cells and the next morning I heard a loud whisper. It was Commander Jim Stockdale, the senior Navy POW. He was in the cell across the hall and he instructed me to remove the transom above the door, allowing us to see each other.

Now Air Wing Commanders are normally around 40 years old. Here was a man who looked at least 75, totally grey beard, deep sunken eyes, black rings around his eyes, grey pallid skin. I said, "Holy smokes, how long have you been here?" This was the end of December. He said, "Since September." And I thought, "Oh man."

Stockdale instructed me to oppose everything they attempted to do to me, to the point of suffering permanent physical damage or until I began to lose my mental faculties. Then lie, cheat, steal, do whatever I had to do to minimize their gain. He gave me a code they used to communicate by tapping on the wall. Soon I learned that he was absolutely right. You weren't going to be able to totally stand up to a hardline code of conduct position. They had means of extracting from you just about anything that they wanted. One guy told me, "You know, at one point, if they had brought my mother in and told me to shoot her, I probably would have."

The Vietnamese were very skilled at their torture methods. About once a month, I'd be called in for an interrogation session where I would get the harangue of the day. I would sit on a little wooden stool, which was very uncomfortable after a few hours. When the harangue was finished, the interrogator would ask me for something -- a statement opposing the war, a letter to my congressman, a letter to the troops in South Vietnam, urging them to quit fighting. If I didn't give it to them, I went back for another torture session until I did give them something, which we all did. There was no choice.

I was in solitary confinement for six months and became very proficient in using our tap code on the walls. We ate twice a day. Each meal was a bowl of watery vegetables, maybe two or three little chunks of turnip or pumpkin, and either a plate of rice or a little loaf of French bread. I lost 50 pounds within the first six months I was there.

We were given a couple pairs of shorts and t-shirts, a pair of long trousers and a long sleeve shirt made of light cotton. The weather could get down to freezing, so we would get quite cold. We had two blankets. The thing they gave us that helped us the most was a mosquito net. At times, the mosquitoes were so thick we could barely see a wall six feet away from us.

I had a little straw mat, ***one straw thick***, which was my mattress on a concrete pad. Often the beds had a set of leg irons at one end where they could lock us down. We had guys that lived for up to six months locked in a set of leg irons with their hands tied behind their back. And that's how we lived.

After several weeks, they took me to a hospital to remove the bullet from my neck. It was like a 1920's vintage operating room. They laid me down on the operating table and turned on a big set of lights above it. It was December, and I'd been cold with practically no sleep for weeks, so I immediately fell asleep on the warm table. They took the bullet out of my neck without anesthetic and I never knew it. They put salve on my burns. That's all they did. I dripped blood and pus for six months, and they wouldn't let me wash the whole time. They just let it fester.

My family didn't know I was alive for the first four years. After my plane went down, I was listed as MIA. Finally, I was allowed to write a letter home. I received 13 letters while I was over there, all in the last three years.

[*Comments from Ray's sister, Lou Shelley*: "When Ray was shot down, my oldest brother and I were no longer living at home; my parents lived alone. I can only imagine how difficult things were for them, not knowing whether Ray was alive. Fortunately, their rural farming community held them up and supported them in many ways. We had a family observance each December 22nd, the day Ray was shot down. His absence was felt acutely, but privately, by each of us on those anniversaries. My father died before my mother received confirmation that Ray was a POW, so that news was happy but somehow sad at the same time."]

Passing Time

As time went on, they put more of us together. Once we were in larger cells, we started getting more organized. We had classes and anybody who knew anything on a topic taught it. We told movies for entertainment. We decided they'd be made-for-TV-movies and those of us that didn't know much about movies wrote the TV commercials. I taught agriculture and wrestling and we had wrestling matches. I also taught music, so we had choirs and church services. And we put on some musical productions including *Oklahoma*. It was fun. Somebody could always come up with the next set of lyrics.

So, we made life a little better as time went along. In September 1969, their president, Ho Chi Minh, died and their policy on the treatment of prisoners began to change. Most of the torture sessions ceased. A lot of the interrogation stopped. They left us alone and we started eating a little better. But every now and then something would tee them off. We could tell how the war was going by the mood they were in.

Coming Home

I lived in eleven different camps including one on the China border for several years. Finally, one night in the fall of 1972, they moved us back down to Hanoi where we learned about a B-52 bombing campaign in downtown Hanoi. They put us in cells according to when we were shot down and told us that we would be going home. They didn't tell us when. Then one day they came in and opened the doors of all the cells of the Hanoi Hilton and said, "You go outside."

We formed up in military formations with our senior guy in front and reported in as a military group. We were told that the war had ended, and our release was part of the agreement. That was January 27, 1973, the day the Paris Peace Accords were signed. On February 12th, the first 200 prisoners were released. Before daylight, they put us on buses and took us to the Hanoi airport where we sat until about three in the afternoon. Finally, three C-141s flew in.

We lined up in two rows. The first to board were the sick and wounded. Then we boarded by shoot-down date. One by one we walked up to a red line on the tarmac where a Vietnamese officer read our name. We stepped over the line and an American Air Force colonel checked off each man's name. Every prisoner had an American escort officer who hustled us onto the plane. Once on board and airborne we were very subdued, not certain they wouldn't shoot us down, until our pilot announced we were *feet wet* (over the water). At that point the whole plane erupted. *[See photo below.]*

Above: FEET WET! Alcorn is front row center.

Left: Alcorn with a very happy mother and young niece.

We flew to Clark Airbase in the Philippines and were taken to the Air Force hospital. They were concerned about what to feed us and what we could handle without getting sick, and they came up with some kind of stew. That was the first of our revolts. We said *"NO, we want breakfast!"* So, they changed course. We were going through the food line and the cook asked the guy in front of me, "How many eggs would you like?" And Leroy said, "You can start with that dozen in your left hand." Leroy ate 19 eggs that night.

After three days we were flown back to the states. I was returning to Bethesda Naval Hospital in Washington DC, so I flew into Andrews Air Force Base and a Marine helicopter flew me around downtown Washington. I was met by my family at Bethesda Naval Hospital. The tour of Washington's monuments at night was an exhilarating and perfect way to come home!

Reflection

I was sustained during those long years in prison by my faith in God, faith in my government, and faith in my fellow countrymen. I knew I had not been nor would ever be forgotten. Upon my repatriation, I was overjoyed to find that these faiths which gave me so much help and comfort were not figments of my imagination but were very true and real.

Captain Ray Alcorn holding the tin mug he received when he arrived at the Hanoi Hilton. He drinks a toast twice a year on December 22nd and February 12th – his shootdown and release dates.

Aftermath

After three months at Bethesda Naval Hospital and another three months on leave, Ray Alcorn returned to active duty. His subsequent assignments included serving as an instructor at the A-7 training squadron, as Operations Officer for Strike Fighter Squadron 83, and as the Executive Officer and then Commanding Officer of Training Squadron 25 at Chase Field, Texas. Next, on the staff of the Deputy Chief of Naval Operations for Air Warfare, Alcorn was head of the Tactical Air Training Branch and then Chief of Staff for

Captain Ray Alcorn, USN

the Chief of Naval Air Training at Corpus Christi, Texas. Captain Alcorn was Commanding Officer of Naval Air Station Fallon, Nevada, until his final assignment as Dean of Students at the Naval War College in Newport, Rhode Island from June 1990 until his retirement in 1992.

Ray and his wife, Karen, moved to North Carolina full-time in 2006. "Karen is the light of my life." The Alcorns and their terrier, Scooter, enjoy the beauty and solitude of their lake and mountain views.

Ray's first Silver Star citation (of 2) reads:

For conspicuous gallantry and intrepidity while interned as a Prisoner of War in North Vietnam. Upon being captured in December 1965, his captors, ignoring international agreements, subjected him to extreme mental and physical cruelties in an attempt to obtain military information and false confessions for propaganda purposes. Through his resistance to those brutalities, he contributed significantly toward the eventual abandonment of harsh treatment by the North Vietnamese.... By his determination, courage, resourcefulness, and devotion to duty, he reflected great credit upon himself and upheld the highest traditions of the Naval Service and the United States Armed Forces.

POW reunion and a return to Hanoi. Ray Alcorn and fellow POWs at the Maison Centrale, Hanoi -- aka Hoa Lo Prison, or the Hanoi Hilton (by U.S. prisoners of war.) Ray is second from the right.

Forty-Five Years Later, a Remarkable Reconnection

The night that Ray Alcorn returned to the U.S. after his ordeal in North Vietnam, USMC 1st Lt. Hale Irwin was waiting in a helicopter on the tarmac at Andrews AFB, assigned to fly Commander Alcorn the short distance to Bethesda Naval Hospital. Irwin was a member of Marine Helicopter Squadron One, the team responsible for the transportation of the president and vice president of the United States and other VIPs and dignitaries, as directed by the Marine Corps and White House Military Office. Many years later, he wrote about the experience in his blog, Checking My Six.

My Most Memorable Mission

The most memorable mission I flew in the CH-46, or in any aircraft for that matter, took place when the Prisoners of War were released from North Vietnam. These men were flown from Hanoi to Clark Air Force Base in the Philippines. From there they were flown to bases near their homes in the United States. I was the aircraft commander waiting late at night at Andrews Air Force Base for the return of a Navy commander who had spent seven years in the Hanoi Hilton and other POW camps.

After the briefest welcome as he stepped off the Air Force jet, he boarded our "46", MX-19. He shook our hands and we welcomed him home. I recall that he was cold, having not an ounce of natural insulation left on his body, so I lent him my flight jacket. With tears in my eyes I lifted off the tarmac at Andrews and headed toward D.C.

Hale Irwin going out for four-plane formation training

I called Washington Tower and requested clearance for the helicopter route to Bethesda Naval Hospital. I told them that Commander Alcorn was on board, returning from seven years as a prisoner of war. The response was: *"Nighthawk-19 you are cleared anywhere you want over Washington. Welcome the Commander home from all of us in Washington Tower."*

This was unprecedented in a region of numerous restricted areas and busy commercial traffic. We gave our hero a beautiful flight across Washington, an unbelievable sight at night from a slow moving helo flying at 1,000 feet. If I was not choked up enough, I was really in tears after we landed on the Bethesda helo pad. He thanked us again, returned my jacket and stepped off the bird into the arms of his family. Home at last, after seven years in Hell!

I have thought about the commander and this flight all my life. Unfortunately, I threw away my logbooks which had become mildewed, and I forgot the commander's name. Forty-five years after this special flight, I was sorting through boxes in my closet which included letters to my dad from college and from my time in the Marines. To my joy, I found a letter which describes that memorable night, including Commander Alcorn's name. I went on-line and found Michel Robertson's article in the *Transylvania Times*. Ray and I were able to connect and relive the evening that we flew from Andrews at 1,000 feet, viewing the White House, illuminated monuments and the Potomac River on our way to Bethesda Naval Hospital. At long last, I was able to tell him how much that flight has meant to me – the most memorable flight of my career.

Capt. Hale Irwin, USMC

Hale Irwin, biking enthusiast, 2019

Polecat Flight, 1969. Irwin squatting on the wing near the number 4.

Welcome Home, Brother

RAY PAVLIK
Choreography on Deck of the USS Kitty Hawk

Ray Pavlik, San Diego, 1965

Choreography has been defined as "a sequence of movements of physical bodies." To Ray Pavlik, an 18-year-old Navy jet mechanic aboard the supercarrier USS *Kitty Hawk* CVA 63, the non-stop operations of launching and recovering aircraft were choreographed maneuvers.

Young Ray Pavlik had not heard of Vietnam when he graduated from high school in 1964 and enlisted in the Navy. "I wanted to get as far away from Cleveland as I could." His proficiency in machines led him to mechanics school in Memphis, and then to Miramar, California. In January 1965, Ray was assigned to VF-213, the Black Lions, a squadron of 112 men, including pilots, who flew and maintained twelve Phantom F-4 jet fighters capable of going anywhere, at any time. Their main station was aboard the USS *Kitty Hawk*.

During their time on shore, the squadron spent a month in the Nevada desert where the pilots practiced bomb runs and simulated carrier landings. One time, a plane stalled and crashed. The RIO (radar intercept operator) was able to eject, but the pilot was not. "I was assigned to identify the engine parts where they landed, which spread out over a football field. There's not much left when a plane hits the ground at 600 mph."

Ray's first cruise introduced him to the hazards of life aboard a carrier. While en route to Hawaii, a sailor fell overboard. As the ship spun to the starboard side to avoid sucking the sailor into the screws, a helicopter crew member fell over the side. Only one of the sailors was rescued. On another occasion, while refueling at sea, an explosion in the carrier's main engine room filled the lower passageways with thick black smoke. "We went to general quarters as the watertight hatches were locked down. I happened to be in the forward galley, unaware of what was happening, unable to see out the porthole. The fire caused heavy damage, killed three crewmen and injured 48 others."

The *Kitty Hawk* was a floating city. Sitting 60 feet out of the water, drawing 40 feet, the carrier weighed 80,000 tons, and spanned almost 1,100 feet long and 300 feet wide, with four catapults, three elevators, 5,000 men, two helicopters, and 12 squadrons of jets, more than 120 planes. The flight deck, where the planes took off and landed, covered more than four-and-a-half acres.

During take offs, or launches, each plane was connected to one of four catapults on the flight deck and catapulted into flight by a combination of its own power and steam

USS Kittyhawk in the South China Sea

pressure. During landings, or recoveries, the pilot snagged the plane's tail hook on one of four cables stretched across the flight deck. The correct amount of steam pressure was applied to allow the cable to unwind slightly but ensure an abrupt halt before the plane went off the end of the flight deck.

Amidst the roar of the jet engines, what might have appeared to be chaos and confusion on the flight deck were precisely organized operations, coordinated by professionals. Continuous momentum on deck required constant vigilance, and lives depended on accuracy and teamwork. Around the clock, large numbers of diversified specialists and technicians worked tirelessly to execute safe and effective launch, recovery and maintenance operations.

Catapults and arresting gear were made ready for the safe launch and recovery of aircraft. Different color shirts worn by crew members defined their responsibilities. *Yellow shirts*, plane handling specialists, assigned each aircraft a position on deck, conveying instructions to the pilots and directing the tractors that moved the planes. *Red shirts*, ordnance crews, loaded bombs onto the aircraft. *Purple shirts* fueled the planes with giant black hoses. And *brown shirts*, known as plane captains, remained on the plane, assuring that it was ready to fly at any given moment and that every moving part in every plane was checked and double-checked. Ray was a brown shirt, or plane captain.

Ray was a plane captain (brown shirt). Each plane had two plane captains one of whom was always with the aircraft.

Ray on deck, preparing F-4 Phantoms for launch.

Two brown shirts were assigned to every plane. Unless the plane was flying, one of the two was always in attendance, and sometimes both. "We worked 12 to 24 hours on the plane." Before each launch, the deck was spotted (planes moved to their assigned positions) by the tractors on deck. Plane captains stayed in the plane to apply the brakes until it was chained down, then continually checked the gauges, resupplied oxygen, and assured there was no damage to the fuselage. As planes took off and landed, yellow shirts repositioned them for the next launch. Every time a plane catapulted into the sky, those remaining on deck would be repositioned, moving toward the catapult.

"We fastened each plane down with up to 15 chains because the ship never stopped rolling. We were always hauling chains around. When the pilot came on deck, I'd strap him in, connect the power and hose to crank the two engines, and take him through his test. Then I'd unchain my plane, throw everything in a bag, and walk to the side. Sometimes it was tough getting across the deck when all the planes were moving into position to launch. Often, they were less than a foot apart, with wings up.

"On my third cruise I was more involved in the mechanics of the planes. I was able to chain down the planes on the back deck, start them up and run them through their course from idle to afterburner." (Afterburner is an additional component added to some jet engines, its purpose being to provide a temporary increase in thrust.) "The power is unreal. The plane just wants to take off."

During the Tet Offensive, the *Kittyhawk* spent more than 60 days offshore. "It was the heaviest bombardment that we experienced. Every plane that was available was launched. There were 120 planes and 60 would take off at a time. They went out, dropped their bombs, and returned within an hour and a half. As planes landed, those that needed maintenance were taken down to the hanger bay and others were brought up in one of three elevators. The yellow shirts put them in position for the next go-around." Night and day, planes moved through an intricate routine of positioning, launching, dropping their bombs, recovery, and preparing for the next launch. "In a crew of 5,000, everybody had his job. Everybody knew what he had to do to make this thing go. That's what was so amazing."

Ray's USS *Kittyhawk* cruise book describes the scene vividly:

> *"The deck is a blur of motion, of sound, of heat waves, of noise and colors moving continuously, as in a kaleidoscope. In clouds of steam, enveloped in noise and heat, the sleek craft pointed their noses down the deck as, with a crack and a roar, they were flung skyward. Behind each, another waited."*

"On one occasion, I had unchained my plane and was walking across the deck, jets moving all around me. I ducked underneath a plane to get to the other side. Just then, the yellow shirt started moving the plane. I was behind the two jet engines at that time. I hit the deck and threw down my bag of chains to hold on to and hide behind. They're quite heavy. The initial gust of power off the two jet engines rolled me toward the A1's on the fantail. I was able to get away quickly as the jet moved beyond me."

On deck, F-4 Phantoms, wings up, stand ready to launch a major strike.

Not all crews returned from their missions. "In hostile waters our jets would sit on the catapult manned and ready. On one such night, I sat with our pilot and RIO, shooting the breeze. That night they were called, and they didn't return. I was told their plane exploded. It was very disheartening. On my three tours with the *Kitty Hawk*, pilots and radar operators sustained the most casualties."

The USS *Kittyhawk* played a significant role in Vietnam, conducting combat operations. *Kittyhawk* received the Navy Unit Commendation for exceptionally meritorious service of her crew during her Vietnam deployment. It reads: *"The officers and men of Kitty Hawk displayed undaunted spirit, courage, professionalism and dedication to maintain their ship as a fighting unit under the most ardent operating conditions to enable her pilots to destroy vital military targets in North Vietnam despite intense opposition and extremely adverse weather conditions."*

Today Ray is a member of the VFW, American Legion and the Vietnam Vets Motorcycle Club. He and his wife Joni are volunteers and docents at the Veterans History Museum of the Carolinas.

Ray rides with the Vietnam Vets Motorcycle Club.

Joni and Ray Pavlik are active volunteers at the Brevard Music Center and the Veterans History Museum of the Carolinas.

Jimmy G. McKinney

Artilleryman Travelling with The Big Red One

*U.S Army, 1st Infantry
Division shoulder patch*

North Carolina native Jimmy McKinney was working at a paper plant when he received his draft notice in May 1966. "I'd been married about three years, with no children. I preferred it to be me rather than kids just out of high school who hadn't had a chance to live. There were a lot of us from Transylvania County. It was the largest draft since the Korean War, taking guys that were married. They called us the *old guys*, because we were twenty-four and twenty-five. We didn't know whether we'd be coming back. It was by the grace of God that we did come back."

Basic training during July and August at Fort Jackson, South Carolina, was an appropriate preparation for a young man soon to be struggling through the dense, humid jungles of Vietnam. "It was unbelievably hot. If the temperature reached a certain point, they allowed us to unblouse our fatigues from our boots, so we didn't pass out and need to be carried back to the barracks. The climate prepared us for Vietnam."

Not Your Father's Howitzer

McKinney was trained in artillery and sent to Fort Sill, Oklahoma, for Advanced Individual Training (AIT) on the M114 155mm howitzer. During WWII, the 155mm howitzer, nicknamed *Long Tom*, was a towed artillery weapon. Self-propelled (SP) artillery guns debuted in Vietnam, replacing the towed howitzers. The tactical advantages of the SP system were greater mobility and flexibility. The gun could stop at the desired location and begin functioning immediately, then quickly move to a new location before its position could be located.

The trip to South Vietnam was long and arduous for McKinney. The battalion travelled by train from Oklahoma to Oakland, where they boarded a ship to Vietnam. "We travelled for a month through the Pacific, stopping in various places and assuming all sorts of duties to keep us active. The ship stopped for one night in Okinawa, where 5,000 troops disembarked. My battalion continued to Vietnam. I don't do well on water, and I had an entire month of seasickness. To make matters worse, we left Okinawa right after a hurricane had hit. The ship was pitching and rolling, and waves were crashing onto the deck. I don't like to remember it."

Although it was a relief to set foot on terra firma in Vietnam, the troopers were concerned that they had reached Vietnam weeks before their weapons and equipment arrived. "It was scary. We were headed for the jungle without our weapons. We were at the mercy of others to guard us until our equipment arrived."

The Big Red One

McKinney was assigned to the 1st Battalion of the 27th Artillery, a 155mm self-propelled M109 howitzer battalion, based at Dau Tieng, in support of the Army's 1st Infantry Division, officially nicknamed *The Big Red One* after its shoulder patch. Also known as The Fighting First, the 1st Infantry Division has seen continuous service since its organization during World War I. "The 1st Infantry Division was on foot in the jungle, scouting out Charlie. When they got into dangerous situations where they needed more fire power, they called in the gun sections as well as the Air Force."

McKinney's howitzer battalion was always on the move. "We might spend a half-day in one location, then travel to wherever the 1st Infantry Division needed us next. We loaded our ammo onto 5-ton track vehicles and quickly got in ranks to move out." Often the artillery group would travel all day, building sleep bunkers at night before they could finally rest. The travel-weary soldiers filled sandbags with dirt and covered them with PSP (pierced steel planking used on Air Force landing strips) as a roof, leaving openings to fire if necessary. "It was frustrating because we were exhausted, but we didn't want to sleep on the ground and get mortared or injured from artillery that was off course."

Firing a Howitzer

As a Specialist 4th Class, McKinney drove the howitzers and served as assistant gunner. In Vietnam there were six gun sections in the battalion with three men on each gun: the gunner, the assistant gunner and the ammo man. Different fuses were used on the projectiles, such as a point detonator or a fuse timed to go off in the air. Howitzers shoot upward and often gunners are unable to see their targets. "We never knew until the mission came down exactly what charge we were firing, getting all our reports from the forward observer."

155mm howitzer projectiles travelled 13 miles.

The 155mm howitzer fired separate-loading bagged-charge ammunition with up to seven different propelling charges, from 1 to 7. Projectiles were about 100 pounds and travelled roughly 13 miles with the maximum seven charge. "You'd load the projectile and use the size charge for the distance that you wanted to fire. The ammo fit into the tubing just right, and we inserted the powder right behind it, with a little primer. When they called for fire, we'd jerk the lanyard and the projectile was on its way. Spotters directed our fire power, giving us different coordinates and azimuths to keep us on target.

"The bombing went on all night. It was nothing to fire 200-300 rounds. Our howitzers were targets, but usually there was infantry on our perimeter that protected us. Trees would fall as the little tanks continuously fired into the jungle, clearing a path in no time."

Driving a Howitzer

The battalion named each of its six howitzers. "I was the designated driver of *Cyclops*." McKinney described maneuvering the 32-ton artillery piece made by General Motors. "It had something like an automobile's steering wheel. You could gently turn it and the howitzer would make a big sweeping turn. It was like an automatic transmission.

"We were usually on the main roads with infantry or guys in personnel carriers guarding us while we travelled, so we wouldn't be overrun. And naturally, they had minesweepers. We couldn't travel until they'd cleared the road. We never really knew how long it would take to get to a location. The howitzers were extremely heavy, as were the tracks. They had rubber pads to prevent tearing up the road. But naturally, we did so much travelling that they didn't last very long.

"The roads were mainly dirt, creating a lot of dust until the monsoon season set in. Then they were nothing but mud. We had to be very careful that the howitzers didn't get stuck. If we couldn't get to the infantry because of the mud, they called the Air Force to protect them, dropping napalm bombs. Often, we were so close that we could feel the heat of the bombs. During the monsoon season, we wore our ponchos day and night and slept under mosquito nets to protects us from the swarms of insects. It was awful."

In January 1968, during the Tet Offensive, the heaviest and most sustained fighting of the Vietnam War, The Big Red One was situated close to Cambodia. "Watching the helicopters bring out howitzers and artillery pieces with tracks blown off and white sheets over the bodies brought tears to my eyes. I knew a lot of guys had been blown up. It was terrifying."

Rubber Trees and Banana Plantations

In the Vietnamese countryside, two sights always captured McKinney's interest: rubber trees and banana plantations. "We often stopped on the road near a banana plantation. I must be part monkey because I have always loved bananas. I really wanted to get one, but we couldn't get out of the howitzer. And it was always neat to see the rubber trees which were considered sacred by the Vietnamese people. You didn't shoot at a rubber tree. There was a price to pay because they were prized possessions."

McKinney recalled passing little grass huts as his division travelled through small villages, unable to determine whether they were friendly or dangerous. "It was crazy. These tiny villages had access to American Coca Cola and the villagers would sell us a Coke for a buck. I have no earthy idea how they got them, but many of us bought them."

Respect for the Men in Charge

"We had some great officers. Everyone respected our captain who did everything he could to take care of us. There was no saluting in Vietnam because if Charlie was watching we didn't want anyone to realize who was in command. And the sergeants were terrific. They had a lot of experience under their belts. Back then I was a very heavy sleeper. I could sleep through anything. During a red alert attack with incoming mortars or rifle fire, one sergeant always woke me up so that I made it into the bunker. Our sergeant in command was also a fine man. They sent him back to base camp to return to the States. But the base camp was mortared, and I don't think he made it home."

Home Again

McKinney returned to the United States in March 1968. Because Saigon was under attack, the battalion flew home out of Bien Hoa, flying first to the Philippines and then to Oakland. He remembers the flight fondly. "It was the era of the mini-skirts. Getting on that plane and seeing those stewardesses in miniskirts was mighty nice to us young guys. Good for the eye. We'll leave it at that."

After a delicious steak dinner, compliments of the U.S. Army, and his discharge, McKinney flew into Asheville, NC. Fortunately for Jimmy and his wife, Helen, they did not encounter war protestors. "There weren't any parties for me, and nobody thanked me, but I wasn't treated badly."

"We had planned to go directly to Florida, but I had to go home first. I had a good friend who was a paratrooper who landed on a land mine during his third tour. He didn't make it, so I went home to see his family. Then we went on to Daytona Beach. It was a cold spell, about 65 degrees, and I was freezing to death. I'd been wearing a poncho in 100-degree temperatures with extremely high jungle humidity. In Daytona, I had the heat on and slept under blankets. I don't know how my wife stood it!"

Thirty years ago, McKinney and his son, Brian, visited the Vietnam Veterans Memorial wall in Washington, D.C. "I thought it was a great memorial. It was so well organized, with all those names and dates. I found the name of a friend, Charles King, who was newly married with a pregnant wife when he left for Vietnam. I found Weldon Merrill, my paratrooper friend, and some men I'd been close to. It touches your soul when you see their names on the wall."

Today, Jimmy, a retired electrician, and his wife, Helen, live in Brevard and are active in their church. Jimmy honors his fallen comrades as a member of the Transylvania County Honor Guard. The McKinneys thoroughly enjoy their seven-year-old granddaughter, Samantha Ann, or Sammy. "She has us wrapped around her little finger."

Jimmy posing by the county veterans' memorial after an Honor Guard ceremony, Memorial Day, 2018.

A Band of Brothers

Jimmy McKinney has no regrets. "It was exhausting, but it was worth it. I feel that I was defending our way of life." Like veterans of all wars, McKinney speaks respectfully of his comrades. "They were men I would die for. They were all troopers. They were all brothers."

Purvis James Boatwright, Jr.
Supporting Fellow Marines on the Ground

VMFA 542 Tigers Squadron

When asked about his tour in Vietnam, Purvis "James" Boatwright, Jr. responds with a mixture of enthusiasm and regret. During the war, Boatwright was a Captain in the Marine Corps, serving as a Radar Intercept Operator (RIO) on the F-4 Phantom, a long-range supersonic interceptor aircraft and fighter bomber. His joy of flying conflicts with survivor's guilt, a condition common among those who have served in combat.

A native of Orangeburg, SC, Boatwright graduated from the University of the South in Sewanee, TN, in 1965. Knowing he would soon be drafted, Boatwright joined the U.S. Marine Corps. After attending Officers' Candidate School and The Basic School at Quantico, he was offered the opportunity to attend flight school at Pensacola.

"I figured flying would be the lesser of two evils of being on the ground or in the air."

The Tigers Squadron

Boatwright arrived at Danang air base in 1967, a member of the VMFA 542 Tigers Squadron. Sitting behind the pilot as an RIO, his role was to help manage the battlefield and mission execution. In support of the Marines on the ground, most of the squadron's missions provided close air support for Marine and Army units. The squadron also made night flights at 30,000 feet, dropping bombs as directed by ground control. During his year in Vietnam, Boatwright flew more than 100 missions, sometimes as many as three a day in good weather.

Boatwright (far right) and buddies in Japan on their way to Vietnam. All returned home.

James Boatwright's primary tasks were navigation and communications. "Communications is very important because you can get messed up in a minute. It can get complicated with different parties trying to talk at the same time. You get so you can understand them all, ignoring what you don't need to know.

"An accident on my first day in Vietnam proved instrumental in my flying experience. We were drinking beer and wrestling and I broke my leg. The brass did not think that was funny at all." While recovering, Boatwright was assigned to a job in intelligence where he briefed and debriefed air crews. It was a good experience. "I got the inside scoop on what was happening on the ground and what happened to people when they flew." This assignment offered Boatwright the chance to meet other officers and pilots – relationships that later enabled him to fly planes other than the F-4s.

"All the flights I flew in the F-4 Phantoms were with my squadron. And then I would approach pilots I knew through debriefing. I'd talk to the pilot and say, 'let me go with you sometime.' And they would."

Phantoms: According to Boatwright, the F-4 Phantom was the hottest airplane in the Marine Corps arsenal. "It was the crème de la crème of planes." The Phantom crews' close-support missions sometimes made the difference between life and death for their fellow Marines. According to Boatwright, it was impersonal combat. "We talked to forward air controllers and they'd say, 'We're going to throw smoke out and we want you to drop your bombs 100 yards north of that smoke.' It was always in the middle of the jungle, so we didn't see anything except the trees. We weren't eyeball to eyeball with the enemy."

Skyhawks: Boatwright flew many missions in the TA-4 Skyhawk, a subsonic attack aircraft which performed both close air support and deep strike missions. While the A-4 is a single seat aircraft, the TA-4 (the *T* stands for training) is a two-seater, used in the U.S. for training. In Vietnam the TA-4 was used for surveillance. "My job was to search for targets of opportunity. We flew several hundred miles into North Vietnam, and we were shot at a lot." If the Skyhawk crew located a target, they would call in the Air Force to handle it. The Skyhawk was the plane John McCain was flying when he was shot down in North Vietnam. "I had more fun in the TA-4 than anything else. I hate using the word fun, but in retrospect, it was fun to fly those planes. "

Intruders: On one occasion, Boatwright flew a mission in an A-6 Intruder, an all-weather medium attack aircraft which is very efficient at subsonic speeds. "These were the planes that would drop the ordnance on Hanoi. They'd fly to North Vietnam at night, low level, in between the mountains, often suffering severe damage."

The pilot that Boatwright flew with was highly skilled. "One morning, as we were waiting to take off, we watched as his plane returned from a mission. They'd been all shot up. They only had one main gear and the nose gear down, a wing was partially shot off, and the tail was partially shot off. The ground crew had foamed the first 200 yards of the runway and the A-6 had to catch a wire or they could have crashed and burned. They caught the wire and jumped out. The pilot got the Silver Star for that. It was incredible watching them come in. That shows how good those pilots are."

Boatwright noted that the F-4 was like driving a Porsche, whereas the A-6 was like driving a Cadillac.

Returning Home

Returning to the states, Boatwright encountered recriminations and hostility. "I was in uniform when I got to Columbia, SC. The taxi driver would not take me home, so I had to walk. I had one friend whose brother kicked me out of his house."

He also suffered from survivor's guilt. "I'd be flying, and someone would come up on the radio, a helicopter crew had gone down, and they'd be shouting 'Mayday, Mayday,' and then there was silence. I knew they'd probably been killed. That happened a lot." Boatwright also had several friends who were killed.

"I also felt guilty because our living conditions were relatively luxurious compared to the Marines in the field. We had hot meals every day, showers (albeit cold showers), and we lived in air-conditioned huts, whereas the grunts were hot and filthy, eating c-rats and getting shot at."

Boatwright returned to the states and served as an S-2 Intelligence Officer at Beaufort, SC. After leaving the service in May 1970, he attended the University of Georgia and went on to veterinary school.

Boatwright at home in Transylvania County, NC, 2018

James with helmet in the Vietnam room at the Veterans History Museum.

In 1998 he sold his practice and moved back to Brevard. Today he lives on See Off Mountain on land purchased by his grandmother in the late 1800's. He assists the Humane Society and is a member of the Transylvania County Honor Guard (*above*).

Boatwright is proud to have served his country, but he regrets our intervention in Vietnam. "Why didn't we listen to the French? It made me so angry. If you're fighting a war, you should fight it to win. Vietnam was a political war."

As to his military service, there are no regrets. "I've been to college and to veterinary school. But I'm prouder of being a Marine than anything else. I have nothing but praise for the Marine Corps. And that's why I'm doing this article. It lets me be a Marine again."

Chief Master Sergeant Joe T. Smith (Ret.).
Under Attack Abroad and at Home

Senior Master Sergeant Joe Smith

Korean War Air Force veteran Joe Smith first arrived in South Vietnam in August 1967, flying into Tan Son Nhut Air Base on the outskirts of Saigon. An experienced Airman, Smith was assigned as a Supply Specialist to the Logistical Division of the 377th Supply Squadron, tasked with providing logistical support to the U.S. and South Vietnamese armies.

Life on the air base was relatively safe. "At that time, we were not fired on as much as the Army and the Marines. The Viet Cong would shoot in a 122mm rocket now and then as harassment. We assumed they wouldn't attack the base for fear of retaliation."

Tet Offensive Attack on Tan Son Nhut Air Base

In December and January, the attacks intensified. Rockets were launched against the air base every night. "We determined that rockets were coming from a steeple in a church on the outskirts of Saigon. Because of the political complications of destroying a church, it took five days to get permission from Washington to blow up the steeple."

On January 31, 1968, things came to a head with the beginning of the Tet Offensive. The assault on Tan Son Nhut Air Base included mortar, rocket, and ground attacks. "Just after midnight, the sirens blared, and we knew the base was under attack. Since we'd been in a support role, we were not heavily armed. We just had side arms and M-16s."

Tan Son Nhut Air Base during Vietnam

Smith and several other airmen raced to the warehouse to retrieve heavier weapons. "When we got there, we found that our weapons were still in cosmoline (protective grease) in crates. We weren't prepared for an attack of this size."

Destroyed airplane

As the bombing increased, the Air Force received reinforcements from the 25th Infantry Division and Army helicopter and ground units. The combined forces drove off an estimated 2,500 attackers. "The helicopter gunships flew around the air base all night, protecting our bomb dump and fuel storage sites. The next day we thought, 'Boy did the Army ever save us Air Force guys!'"

Smith noted that the Tet Offensive had a dramatic impact on Air Force operations. "It became apparent that we could be targeted by large enemy forces. Security was greatly enhanced, and the Air Force became much more involved in defending our bases."

Attacks on the Home Front

Smith left Vietnam in August 1968, when the United States was bitterly divided over the country's involvement in Vietnam. Protests were common. Upon their arrival at California's Travis Air Force Base, the GI's were briefed about protests and it was suggested that they change into civilian clothes. "Some guys did, and some didn't. People were protesting everywhere we went."

Smith and two other airmen flew to Chicago to catch a train to Virginia. At the airport, they hailed a taxi to take them to the train station. "The driver knew we were GI's returning from Vietnam. It took an hour to get to the station and he charged us $75." At the train station, the GIs learned it was a 20-minute trip, usually costing $30 for the group. "We were surprised and very upset that we were scammed by a cab driver. This was our introduction back into the United States."

Smith was assigned to Seymour Johnson Air Force Base in Goldsboro, NC, where, the Air Force held a decoration ceremony for returning veterans. "I still remember standing in full dress uniform, receiving the Bronze Star for service to my country, and remembering the suggestion that I change out of my uniform at Travis Air Force Base.

Reflections on the War

"As a career military guy, I can tell you that the Vietnam War will be remembered as the biggest blunder this country has ever made – getting involved in a war with no intention of winning. I think of all the sacrifices made for this war. We all had a different mission. None of us had a choice of what we did or where we went. I'm still bitter about how I was treated when I got home. I guess it's because we felt so betrayed by our countrymen."

After two wars and serving 26 years in the Air Force, Joe retired from HQ Strategic Air Command as a Chief Master Sergeant, the highest enlistment level of leadership. He and his wife, Joan, live in the NC mountains and enjoy volunteering and traveling.

Smith holds a model plane given to him as a very young man by his commanding officer at Langley AFB. Joe became familiar with the seven original astronauts who were required to attend flight training at Langley once a month. Smith worked on the flight line and helped the astronauts into their parachutes.

Welcome Home, Brother

Lt. Col. John K. Barker, USAF (Ret.)

Flying F-4 Phantoms Over Hanoi

Triple Nickel 555th Fighter Squadron

Lt. Col. Barker's story, in his own words.

I received my commission as a 2nd Lieutenant in May 1965. A year earlier, I had graduated from Duke University and had been accepted into the Air Force's Officer Training School (OTS) as a pilot candidate. Following a year of pilot training at Moody AFB, Georgia, I received my wings and was assigned to George AFB, CA, for qualification training in the F-4 Phantom II, with a follow-on combat assignment to Vietnam.

The F-4 is a Mach 2 fighter-bomber with twin afterburning jet engines and is capable of carrying a formidable array of bombs, rockets, missiles, cannon, and other unpleasant stuff. It's a highly complex, versatile, demanding machine, and built like an airborne tank. It carries a crew of two, seated in tandem cockpits.

The war in Southeast Asia was increasing in intensity at this time, so there was a sense of urgency in getting us trained for combat as quickly as feasible. Our instructor pilots at George had recently returned from combat duty, so we profited greatly from the "pearls of wisdom" they passed on to us.

The front seat pilot, or Aircraft Commander (AC), trainees in our class were more senior officers with many years of flying experience, particularly in other fighter aircraft models. Newly minted pilots were basically in a co-pilot role in the aft seat until we gained enough experience and training to upgrade to the front seat. (Air Force policy at the time required that both crewmembers be rated pilots. This changed a few years later, when navigators, rather than pilots only, were assigned as rear-seat crewmembers. Meanwhile, this rear-seat pilot policy caused considerable grumbling among us cocky *young eagles*, but it made sense in many ways.) We were affectionately known as GIBs (Guy In Back). As GIBs we spent most of our time operating the radar, weapons, and navigation systems which gave the F-4 its awesome attack capabilities.

Upon completing the flight qualification course at George, we received our combat assignments. Mine was to the 8th Tactical Fighter Wing (the "Wolfpack") in Thailand. We were given about a week of leave prior to departing the States, so I made good use of the time by courting a young lady named Helen from Los Angeles I'd recently met.

I arrived at Ubon Royal Thai Air Base in February 1967. Our Wing Commander was the legendary Colonel Robin Olds, a ferocious fighter pilot and World War II Ace, who was as inspiring a leader as any young aviator could have wished for. My AC, Captain Joe Higgs, and I were assigned to the 555th Tactical Fighter Squadron, the *Triple Nickle*. It was Air Force policy then that once a pilot completed 100 combat missions over North Vietnam, his tour was complete. The trick was to reach this number while still in one piece. Sadly, many of our squadron mates didn't make it that far.

Capt. Joe Higgs and Lt. John Barker with F-4C Phantom March 1967

The most common missions, and the hairiest by far, were the bombing raids we made into the Hanoi area, reportedly the most heavily defended territory in history. These strikes typically involved 12 to 20 aircraft, each armed with air-to-ground ordnance, air-to-air missiles, extra fuel tanks, and various other hardware items. Preparation for each mission required several hours of target study, pre-flight briefings on weather, intelligence, enemy defenses, weapon settings, delivery parameters, and so on. The amount of planning detail involved for each flight was extensive, but critical to mission success.

Following the briefings, each pilot collected his gear – survival vest, anti-G suit, flight helmet, sidearm, extra water flasks, etc. – and reported to his assigned aircraft on the flight line. After a thorough walk-around inspection of the aircraft and ordnance, we strapped into the cockpit and stood by on the radio for engine start time. With both engines up and running and generators online, we checked all systems to make sure the aircraft and weapons were operating as expected.

Phantoms in a four-ship flight.

Once the entire strike force had started engines and taxied to the runway for takeoff, things got pretty serious. For anyone in the vicinity of the runway the noise level became deafening – imagine the Daytona 500 on steroids. Takeoff was made in two-ship, or *element*, formation, hustling down the runway in full afterburner, accelerating to a lift-off speed of about 160 knots. Two elements would then join up in the air as a four-ship "flight." Each flight of four circled the airfield in close formation, joining up with the other flights, until the entire strike force was formed. Then the whole gaggle climbed to altitude, headed for the airborne tankers, and proceeded with air-to-air refueling. Topping off the fuel tanks as close to the target area as possible was vital, just in case we had to hang around after the strike for longer than expected.

Flying a jet fighter has been whimsically described as "hours and hours of boredom, relieved occasionally by a few moments of stark terror." That's never truer than when the enemy starts shooting at you, as normally happened during interdiction missions against an enemy airfield or munitions factory in the Hanoi area. On rare occasions, we'd enter the target area without opposition, and the raid would go off without a hitch. Most of the time, however, the North Vietnamese would interrupt the strike force with ground-to-air defenses or by airborne intercept with their own fighters. Then all hell would break loose.

To complicate things further, the dive bomb maneuver requires intense and total concentration for 15 to 20 seconds after rolling in on the target. About six parameters (dive angle, air speed, release altitude, etc.) all must be met at precisely the same instant that weapons are released, or else the bombs will probably miss their target. During these few critical seconds, the aircraft is most vulnerable to enemy fire, so the adrenaline rush is at a peak. If just prior to, or especially during, the dive your aircraft was in imminent danger of being hit by air defense artillery or a surface-to-air missile, the wisest move was to break off the attack in favor of saving your own you-know-what.

The commie gunners, of course, knew this very well. This required that you jettison your bombs and any other external stores, break away from the pending threat, ignite the afterburners if necessary, and immediately begin a series of twisting-and-turning, erratic changes in altitude and direction known as *jinking*. It's not very comfortable. If the threat was enemy fighter planes, on the other hand, the occasion called for switching to air-to-air combat mode, or a *dogfight*. This rare opportunity, by the way, is what every self-respecting fighter pilot lives for. I only had one such encounter, but since we were really low on fuel, and the MiG was flying down in the weeds where enemy ground fire was a threat, we had to break it off and postpone our day of fame and glory.

Following the delivery of all ordnance by the strike force, it became a matter of reassembling from our scattered locations around the target area and heading for home, or, in the vernacular, getting the hell out of Dodge. Each crew eventually rejoined its element, two elements rejoined as a flight, and flights rejoined the strike force, all while traveling at warp speed, trying to avoid enemy defenses, and chattering on the radio to determine everyone's status. To a casual observer, this post-attack scene would have probably looked like absolute chaos. But this max performance, high-speed egress dance is exactly what the pilot delights in, and it's how fighter aircraft are designed to perform. The pilot is unleashed for a few incredible moments, and he is given leave to fly like a madman. He may briefly put aside the strict discipline of formation integrity, get some compensation for many monotonous hours of straight-and-level flight, bear his fangs, and take his powerful aerodynamic machine through its paces.

If a crew had taken a severe hit and had to bail out, we tried to pinpoint the exact spot where their parachutes landed in case a search and rescue operation was feasible, or at least to visually confirm that, in the best case, both crew members had punched out of their crippled aircraft successfully. Seeing a squadron mate shot down over enemy territory was the gut-wrenching event that each of us dreaded the most, for understandable reasons.

As frequently happened, however, a stricken aircraft might be coaxed out over the Gulf of Tonkin, before it gave up the ghost and had to be abandoned. The crew could then eject over the water and reasonably expect to be rescued almost immediately. The F-4 was tough enough in many cases to stagger all the way back to base and land safely, even after suffering seemingly catastrophic damage.

But if all turned out okay, and once we were reassembled into formation and safely out of harm's way, the strike force joined up with the KC-135 tanker aircraft for a second refueling. Flight suits were soaked with sweat, muscles ached from high G-force maneuvering, and throats were dry, but we were finally headed home.

Not surprisingly, there were occasional episodes of comic relief. One of my favorites was the day Lt. Bill Harding was initiated into the fraternity. On the morning of his second day on base, he began his week-long Theater Orientation program, completion of which was mandatory (or so he thought) before your first combat mission. A huge strike force that morning was about to start engines and take the runway, but one of the GIBs was suddenly unable to man his aircraft and had to be replaced. Despite Bill's pleas of newcomer status, he was ordered into the vacant cockpit. On his second day on base and first combat mission, Bill was shot down during the mission. He managed to limp out of enemy territory and eject over the water, where he was rescued. He is credited with coining the phrase, as he descended in his parachute, "Sweet Jesus! Only 99 more to go!"

After safely landing from one of these exhausting, four-hour-long missions, and following the post-flight debriefings, we usually made a beeline for the Stag Bar, the location of choice for relieving the day's stress and swapping war stories. If all had gone well, and if each flight had returned without casualties or losses, the celebration was understandably festive. If a crew had scored a MiG kill, the ultimate prize for any fighter pilot, there was absolute bedlam.

It took me eight months to reach the magic goal of 100 missions, and in October I completed my combat tour. I was reassigned to Yokota Air Base, Japan, for a three-year operational tour in the F-4, this time as an Aircraft Commander. Helen and I were married during this tour.

Captain John K. Barker

In 1972, I returned to Ubon for another combat tour. There had been a dramatic shift in the combat environment from when I was there last. The most significant change was in the sophistication of the tactical weapons we were now using. New state of the art laser-guided delivery systems and smart bomb technology had replaced the former generation of ballistic ordnance, and precise, surgical strikes against virtually any target were now the norm. Improved radar and heat-seeking guidance on our air-to-air missiles ensured much greater reliability and effectiveness in virtually any environment.

Even the formidable North Vietnamese missiles and AAA (anti-aircraft artillery) weapons were increasingly vulnerable to our jamming and interdiction systems. We had attained unquestioned air superiority from the very beginning, so enemy aircraft were normally not much of a threat to our strike forces. Bombing operations continued but not on the scale of earlier years.

The former 100 mission policy had been changed by this time, and the required tour length was now one year. Rumors of pending peace negotiations began to spread, and it soon became evident that air operations over North Vietnam would soon come to a halt. I completed my tour in February of 1973 at about the time the Paris Peace Accords were being signed, and received orders to 9th Air Force Headquarters at Shaw AFB, SC.

John Barker

There are few things more exhilarating and memorable than what I experienced in Southeast Asia, and I made it home in one piece, so I have a lot to be thankful for. "

Barker retired in 1985 as a Lieutenant Colonel. In addition to his F-4 and other aircraft assignments, he was an F-16 instructor pilot and squadron commander. Among his decorations are the Distinguished Flying Cross with three oak leaf clusters and the Air Medal with seventeen oak leaf clusters. He and Helen celebrated their 50th wedding anniversary in June.

John Barker holding a helmet worn by F-4 pilots, Veterans History Museum of the Carolinas, 2018.

Welcome Home, Brother

Ervin P. Bridges, Jr.

Walking to War

Combat Infantryman Badge

"What the heck am I doing here? Will this be my last command?" These were Captain Ervin P. Bridges' thoughts as he stood up firing and shouted "Go!" during an operation to break the siege on Khe Sanh, one of the longest and bloodiest battles of the Vietnam War.

A native of Raleigh, NC, Bridges enlisted in the Army the day after his 21st birthday, while in the second semester of his third year at NC State. "I'd wanted to be in the Army since I was six years old. My dad was in WWII and I felt it was my obligation to go into the service." Bridges attended Officer Candidate School (OCS) and was commissioned as a second lieutenant on March 7, 1967.

Light Infantry Brigade

Bridges prepared for the harsh terrain of Vietnam at Jungle Operations Training School in Panama. In mid-October 1967 he was sent to Vietnam, attached to the 199th Light Infantry Brigade, based near Saigon. However, upon his arrival, he was reassigned to the 196th Light Infantry Brigade, 4th Battalion, 31st Infantry Regiment in I Corps, the northernmost provinces in South Vietnam.

On Bridges' first night with the 196th Light Brigade, the commander, a brigadier general, invited him and two other officers to dinner. "He told us that he liked to ease second lieutenants into the job, to give us a chance to get our feet on the ground before he put us out in the field. I think the Army considered second lieutenant the lowest rank in the Army including private 1st class. "A lot of guys fresh out of OCS thought they knew it all. I knew from talks with my dad that I should listen to my sergeants and other seasoned NCO's. That was my mindset and it served me well."

As a platoon leader, Bridges originally oversaw the team's primary mission, protecting fire support bases (FSBs). Later he was responsible for search and destroy missions as a foot soldier.

Walking to War

In Vietnam, Light Infantry Brigades were units of soldiers with no attached tanks or armored personnel carriers. Once the troops were transported to a specific location, they often walked to war, rather than rode to it. The terrain was swamps, rice paddies, tropical jungles and dense forests.

Bridges vividly recalls one night during his first tour. "We were northwest of the Qua Son Valley, about 35 miles south of Da Nang, protecting a firebase called Landing Zone Colt. There were three vills (small hamlets) down the mountain from us: one was pro-Viet Cong, one was pro-government, and the third was a mixture of both. The pro-government village was defended by the Civilian Irregular Defense Group (CIDG), mostly old men and kids holding M-1 rifles taller than they were. One night, the Viet Cong attacked the hamlet with satchel charges, throwing them into the sleeping bunkers. They followed up with flamethrowers, killing 432 people, all men, women and children. From then on, I never had qualms about what we did during the war. It hardens you.

"During search-and-destroy missions, every five or six days a helicopter would bring us a change of clothing, more ammo, mail, and c-rats. Each man would receive 15 meals (three a day), but that weighed more than 25 pounds, a lot of weight for an infantryman, so, we'd break it down to just one meal a day. A day's worth of food was three cookies, hot chocolate, a can of fruit, a can of meat and a can of bread or crackers. We were always hungry. Often we weren't looking for the enemy as much as we were looking for food."

Combat infantrymen had to be self-sufficient, carrying everything with them. During the monsoon season their packs became even heavier. [Photograph from geographicalimaginations, wordpress.com.]

Slogging through rice paddies and jungle terrain, never an easy task, became substantially more difficult with the load each soldier carried. Bridges' personal combat load included a trenching tool, a .45, two combat knives, fifty rounds of ball ammo, three clips for the .45, an M-16 and thirty magazines, 400 rounds of loose ball, 5 c-rat meals, a poncho and poncho liner, canteens, a towel, shaving kit, 6 hand grenades, six-to-ten smoke grenades, trip flares, extra batteries for his radio operator, signal flares, and sometimes extra rounds of machine gun ammo.

"We carried enough junk so that sometimes when we got tired, we'd put our pack down, slide into it and crawl on our hands and knees. We weighed it out one time and we carried 100 pounds of equipment, sometimes running." Bridges' platoon travelled about ten miles a day, depending on the mission.

Bridges recalls one occasion during the Tet Offensive in 1968. "We were moved north to Camp Evans and were attached to the First Cav. Our mission was to support the Marines. They had tried to cut off the enemy's supplies going into Hue and we had to get to them in three days. For 36 hours, we moved night and day, 100 miles total. We didn't wear socks because of trench foot, and we took our boots off at least twice a day to powder our feet. We slept in our boots so we could move quickly if we were hit at night.

"We were doing a lot of night ambushes and combat sweeps every day, walking through mine country and taking occasional casualties. One night, we were called back in by our company commander, who told us we had to get to a designated point by daybreak. He put us at a jog throughout the night. We'd run 50 feet, walk 50 feet, run 50 feet, walk 50 feet."

At daybreak, Bridges' platoon was transported by helicopter to a mountain in the A Shau Valley, a narrow, 25-mile arm of the Ho Chi Minh Trail, which funneled troops and supplies toward Hue and Da Nang. "We became involved in something later called the Battle of the Ridges."

A light infantry platoon from B Company had been sent in to rescue a long-range reconnaissance patrol (LRRP, *pronounced 'lurp'*), a team of seven men who were under fire and fighting for their lives. Bridges' A Company second platoon was to support the now-besieged B Company platoon, along with the rest of A Company. A helicopter dropped his team as the bird hovered about 15 feet above the scrub brush on the side of the mountain. "I knew it wasn't going to be a good day when we ran across enemy commo wire. Also, we thought that we were taking fire from our own gunships, but it turned out to be enemy recoilless fire as we were loading the choppers at the base of the ridge line.

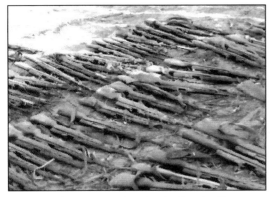

Arms cache recovered in the A Shau Valley

"We moved up and as soon as we got to the crest of the hill, all hell broke loose. The LRRP commander had survived, but the other six men had been killed. There were three bodies left behind and our job was to retrieve them. We got the bodies out under fire and started filtering out the wounded to an LZ cut out just below where we were kicking off our assault.

"We went up and down that hill four times that day and night. We often wondered whether we'd make it. We just decided, 'Well, this is our job.' We just sucked it up. We were there for three days. We started with 40 men and I had 17 at the end."

The Battle of Que Son Valley

"We were flown back to the Que Son Valley and nine days after A Shau, we engaged in another major battle where we went in with 120 men and came out with about sixty.

"We took a small hill overlooking a river where they Hiep Duc and Que Son Valleys joined. We went in thinking that the hill might be protected by an NVA platoon. In fact, it was an old American fire support base with concertina wire, and the whole interior of the mountain was dug out to support the NVA HQ.

"We moved up the hill at 0200 hours. When they opened up on us, 15 of the first 16 men in the column were either killed or wounded within the first five seconds. One of my men was killed six hours earlier as he assisted loading the body of our company medic plus six others wounded when enemy mortar rounds cut them down.

"My RTO (radio telephone operator) was wounded and evacuated as we dug in and gathered our wounded and dead on an LZ just behind a small knoll. Green tracers lit up the night, cutting down all the elephant grass. The NVA landed 430 mortar rounds plus recoilless rifle rounds, while RPGs and grenades rolled down on us in an area about the size of a basketball court. We stopped counting after that, but the mortars continued to fall.

"My RTO jumped off one of the medevacs and rejoined us in the fight as they loaded additional wounded. He was wounded again about four hours later -- his third purple heart in three weeks.

"Such was the strength and character of the men that I fought beside the entire time I was in Vietnam. WWII may claim the title of The Greatest Generation, but the Vietnam vets were stepping on their coattails unrecognized during our ten years of fighting. "

One Tough Guy

"The battalion operations officer was a major. On Thanksgiving day, 1968, some armored personnel carriers (tracks) and a tank were sent out to attack enemy positions in a rice paddy. The major was sitting on the top of his track, issuing orders, when he was shot -- hit in the shoulder and knocked off the track. When he tried to get up, the track behind him ran over him. I thought, 'Well, that's the end of him.' But it wasn't. It just made him mad. We found him sitting in a Jeep, covered with mud and fuming. They bandaged him up and shipped him home."

Home and Back Again

Bridges returned to the United States in October 1968. "I couldn't talk about my tour with my family when I got home, but I was able to talk to my best friend who was home from the Peace Corps. One day I went to visit him at his house. His mother answered the door and called to him, 'Harold, that baby killer is here.' I never went back to that house. I actually had friends who turned their backs on me, so I stayed in the military."

At Fort Bragg, Bridges trained troops and was promoted to Captain. Shortly after that, he was sent back to Vietnam. "On my second tour, I was team commander for a Military Assistance Team, stationed in Hoi An near the South China Sea. Every time we went out to a particular island, we made enemy contact. I was there for four-and-a-half months, until I was wounded."

Hoi An. Capt. Bridges coming ashore from a Buddha boat (with dragon head). Bridges was Senior Mat Team leader during his second tour.

Capt. Ervin Bridges, Xuan Loc 1970, second tour.

Wounded in Action

Bridges earned his Purple Heart on November 1, 1970, when he stepped on a land mine. Fortunately, he was thigh-deep in water, which saved his life. "It crushed the heel of my right foot and broke my ankle in nine places." Despite an approaching typhoon, a squad of Marines carried Bridges out and put him on a Boston Whaler. "I debriefed my province commander that night. But I'd suffered a concussion and had an embolism which put me into a coma. I woke up ten days later on the USS *Sanctuary* on the South China Sea." Bridges spent 12 days in Japan where they stabilized his fever which came from an infection in his foot. He was flown home to Fort Bragg where they cut it open. "It was the size of a basketball, and green, but they were able to save my foot."

Still Serving After All These Years

"The most remarkable aspect of my Vietnam experience was the caliber of the men over there. There were a lot of good soldiers -- draftees, enlisted men, and officers. I can't say enough about them. They always had our backs. That's one thing I've never forgotten. If I can't say anything else about my tours, I respected the people I worked with over there and I respected the job they did."

Ervin and Kathy Bridges and their daughter Erin Bridges Rogers(left), 2018

Bridges was retired out of the military on disability, having served five-and-a-half years in the Army. He married Kathy Stone, his cousin's friend who had written to him while he was in Vietnam and visited him while he was recovering from his injury. "She's a great person, and she's sassy. In fact, that's her nickname. She probably saved my life."

As a loan officer, Bridges eventually moved to Brevard, NC where he worked at First Citizen's Bank. Today, he and Kathy are retired and enjoy the tranquility of their mountain home.

Bridges continues to serve his country and his community as a member of the Transylvania County Honor Guard and a volunteer fireman for the Little River Fire District.

Bridges (back left) receiving a Quilt of Valor, 2018. Other Vietnam veterans in this book: Curtiss Poteat (standing, far right) and Mike Di Rocco (standing 2nd from right).

Ervin after an Honor Guard ceremony

CDR. WILLIAM E. ROBERTSON, CEC, USN (RET.)
Seabees' Can-Do Motto Tested in Vietnam

Ensign William E. Robertson

Navy Lt. Cdr. William E. "Bill" Robertson experienced cultural shock in 1969 when he traded his duty station on the sands of Pearl Harbor for the sands of Red Beach, South Vietnam. In 1969, Robertson, an engineer in the U.S. Navy Civil Engineer Corps assigned to Naval Construction Battalion 62 (CB, or *Seabees*), left behind a wife and three young daughters. As Operations Officer, he would be supervising all construction activities of his 800-man battalion.

Seabees were trained for combat as well as construction, a tribute to their motto, *We build, we fight*, symbolized in their logo of a bee holding a wrench, hammer and machine gun.

The Seabees motto is Construmus Batumius:
We Build, We Fight

Viet Cong Techniques Challenge Seabee Construction

The Seabees played an important role in Vietnam. They dug ditches, built roads and bridges, sank wells, and constructed completely self-sustaining South Vietnamese naval bases. During the peak of the Vietnam conflict, Seabees numbered 25,000 men in 22-two battalions, two regiments, two maintenance units and scores of civic action teams. Nearly $100 million worth of construction was completed by the Seabees, a 3 million man-day effort with construction ranging from logistical complexes to Special Forces camps in remote regions. [*Source: Seabees Museum*]

Robertson directed operations primarily in Dong Ha and Da Nang. "The area around Da Nang was probably the most dangerous place we worked due to the large number of Viet Cong."

Seabees at work in I Corps. "We built bridges by day so they could blow them up at night."

Building roads and bridges was extremely dangerous and frustrating. One of the primary factors of building a road is water control. In Vietnam that meant that in many places Seabees had to build the road higher than the surrounding ground, leaving a shoulder exposed at the side of the road. "Like today's insurgents in the Middle East, the Viet Cong were very clever with their explosives. They dug small cavities in the edge of the road and inserted mines constructed of something that contained very little metal, which weren't easily detected by our minesweeping crews. The mine might not go off the first time a truck drove over it, or the second or the 10th or the 100th time, but eventually it blew up and destroyed a section of road as well as the vehicle and, too often, the operator."

Bridge construction was equally challenging. The Viet Cong equipped small rafts with explosives and set them to float down the river. The rafts were built so that when they hit a bridge, they stuck there until they blew up. "We used to say that we built bridges by day so the enemy could blow them up at night." Building and rebuilding roads and bridges surrounded by guerilla warfare was stressful and disheartening, especially with Seabee loss of life. "Equipment operators suffered the largest number of casualties. Our heavy equipment often set off the mines. The trigger might just be a piece of bamboo that had been bent, and the wires wouldn't make contact until the bamboo finally broke. If you put a heavy piece of equipment on it, a jeep or small truck, there it goes."

Seabees Greatest Danger: Land Mines

"A helicopter transporting a Marine general was preparing to land when an explosion detonated near the landing site. A Jeep with two Marines went to meet the general and drove over a mine, detonating it. One of our Seabees was near the Jeep and both Marines and our man, Nelson Hyler, were killed. Sadly, I had interviewed Hyler on his arrival at the battalion only several days previously.

Construction equipment mangled after driving over a land mine. Remarkably, the driver survived.

"At first, those of us within the vicinity of the explosion did not realize it came from a mine. Our equipment operators had been keeping their eyes on a small village nearby and suspected it might be a Viet Cong shelter. Some of the Seabees wanted to invade the village to punish the residents. The senior petty officers and I convinced them not to do this, although we agreed that in Vietnam, discerning a friend from an enemy was often impossible. Shortly thereafter we discovered the real cause of the explosion was the mine.

"By the nature of our mission, Seabees suffered more injuries and death from mines than from any other cause. We did experience mortar and rocket attacks on our camps, especially at night. Our battalion chaplain and I shared a hooch and we had a foxhole under the floor, large enough to hold a cot for each of us. When an attack on the camp occurred, we lifted the cover of the foxhole and resumed our naps on the cots, often sleeping through the attack until reveille."

Transitioning Home

Seabees encountered fewer problems transitioning back to the states than veterans of other branches. "Because Seabees typically deployed and returned as a unit, we were not isolated in the larger community and thus avoided much of the anti-military criticism experienced by other branches."

Robertson described one transition difficulty common to most military families. "During the Vietnam War, most of the spouses at home were women. While we were away, our wives assumed responsibilities for all household decisions. When we returned, we automatically picked up where we'd left off, often with the attitude, 'Big Daddy's home, let me handle it.' Our wives knew that we'd soon be leaving again and said 'No, Big Mama's got this!' For many couples, this was a source of friction."

Bill Robertson's post-Vietnam Naval career included Procurement Officer for the Naval base at Diego Garcia and Planning Officer at NAVFAC headquarters in Washington, D.C., preparing military construction submissions to Congress. During Robertson's final overseas billet in Saudi Arabia, he served as an advisor to the Saudi Navy. After two years in the Office of the Secretary of Defense at the Pentagon, Bill retired as a Commander in 1985. He still enjoys construction projects, but of a more subdued nature!

Bill holding a chunk of ice from a glacier while on a trip to Iceland in 2017.

JOSEPH A. SANSOSTI

The Fiercely Fought Battle of Dai Do

The Magnificent Bastards Insignia

Public attitudes toward Joseph "Joe" Sansosti and his fellow Marines have changed significantly since 1968, when Sansosti arrived in San Francisco from Da Nang just two days before Christmas. He and other returning war veterans almost despaired of catching a final flight home. Hundreds of students mingled with the soldiers, vying for stand-by seats. Nobody was willing to give up a seat to a Vietnam War veteran who had just spent 18 hours on a flight to the states.

In 1967, 18-year old Joe Sansosti left high school to join the Marines. "My daddy said to my brother, 'That dummy doesn't even know there's a war going on.' I just wanted to do something different."

After boot camp and combat infantry training at Camp Pendleton, California, Sansosti arrived in Vietnam on December 5, 1967. "I got to Danang and they sent me north to join the 2nd Battalion, 4th Marines (BLT 2/4), Hotel Company. We called it Heartbreak Hotel." BLT 2/4 is an infantry battalion, nicknamed the *Magnificent Bastards.*

In December 1967, BLT 2/4 embarked on the USS *Iwo Jima*, off the coast of Vietnam on the South China Sea. The battalion was reinforced with artillery, tanks and other combat support units. In January 1968, the North Vietnamese Army (NVA) and the South

Vietnamese Viet Cong initiated the Tet Offensive, a campaign of strikes on military command posts throughout South Vietnam. The Tet Offensive resulted in an increase in fighting along the DMZ. "We were sent to places that were really hot, such as Khe Sanh, Cam Lo, Con Thien (the rock pile), Quang Tri, and Camp Big John, flying in and out of Mai Xa Chanh. Then we encountered Dai Do."

Lt. Col. William Weise was the battalion commander of the Magnificent Bastards during the Battle of Dai Do (*die-doe*) -- a three-day period during which his battalion landing team faced incredible odds against the 320th NVA Division. Now a retired Brigadier General, William 'Wild Bill' Weise described the engagement as follows:

> Near the end of April 1968, one of the most fiercely fought but little-known battles of the Vietnam war pitted Marines of Battalion Landing Team 2/4, the Magnificent Bastards, against the North Vietnamese 320th Division. It took place on a little piece of terrain approximately 1½ miles northeast of the headquarters of the 3rd Marine Division which was in the Dong Ha combat base. The fighting extended over a three-day period.
>
> This is the only engagement of the entire Vietnam conflict where a single reinforced battalion-sized Marine unit, with less than 1,000 fighting men, supported by intense naval gunfire, fought head-to-head with a division-sized unit of between 6,000 to 10,000 regular NVA soldiers who were augmented with 600 guerillas and who were supported by artillery on the demilitarized zone.

The Battle of Dai Do

On April 30, 1968, a U.S. Navy utility boat motored down the Bo Dieu River, just south of Vietnam's demilitarized zone. As it approached the convergence with the Cua Viet River, NVA troops, hidden along the shoreline, fired rocket-propelled grenades at the U.S. ship. One sailor was killed, and several others were injured. The attack was part of the NVA's plan to demolish the 3rd Marine Division's headquarters at Dong Ha and to

Joe Sansosti at the Cua Viet River

take control of the two rivers, cutting off supply routes to all Marine bases near the DMZ.

After the attack, 2nd Battalion Commander Weise ordered Sansosti's Hotel Company to clear the small village of An Lac where the attack had occurred. In its attempt to cross a stream to reach An Lac, Hotel Company came under intense fire from the nearby villages of Dong Huan and Dai Do. With support from Marine artillery batteries, Hotel Company managed to secure Dong Huan. "The South Vietnamese (ARVN) were supposed to help but they evaporated. It was like that old saying: 'We've got some carbines for sale. They were never fired and dropped only once.'"

Meanwhile, Marine Bravo, Echo, Golf, and Foxtrot companies encountered intense, close-combat activity as they attempted to secure other small villages, making their way to Dai Do. "We had never been up against a force of that size. That's what was different from all the other battles we'd experienced which were basically hit-and-run. We didn't know it at the time, but this was an enemy division of close to 10,000 men."

During the fighting in Dai Do and surrounding villages, the Marines engaged in battle tactics like those used in WWII. At Dai Do, fighting was often hand-to-hand, bunker-to-bunker, in open farmland and over hedgerows, often more like Normandy than anything seen in Vietnam.

Over the course of three days, the relentless onslaughts of 600 Marines, assisted by air and artillery strikes, held fast and managed to gain ground at Dai Do, Dong Huan, and

An Lac in the face of overwhelming odds. "I'll never forget lying in a rice paddy with jets coming down so close to us that I thought, 'You've got to be kidding me!' The Air Force forward observer was calling the shots which were amazingly accurate." Ultimately, the NVA retreated to the DMZ.

Marines were outnumbered 10-1 at the Battle of Dai Do.

Wounded in Action

After Dai Do was secured, the Marines of Hotel Company were ordered to move to two villages to the northwest. The NVA furiously counterattacked and surrounded H Company which was now down to 50 men. Hearing the cries for help, Echo Company, under the command of Capt. James E. Livingston and down to 30 men, rushed to assist Hotel. Marines everywhere cleared hundreds of bunkers, holes and positions, fighting hand-to-hand much of the time. Livingston was later awarded the highest military decoration, the Medal of Honor.

"It was unreal how many NVA there were. They were everywhere we looked. During one counterattack, my best buddy Jerome Pryor and I were in a trench, surrounded by the enemy. We couldn't see any of the other guys from our platoon. An unknown second lieutenant came up, grabbed us by the collars and said 'Y'all get on closer up there.' I thought, 'I can see just fine from right here.'

"However, my buddy Pryor started moving and I said, 'Damn, I can't let you go by yourself.' So, we moved forward and dove into a bomb crater. Enemy fire was fierce. After one explosion, shrapnel hit my back. It felt like it was on fire. As Pryor was putting a bandage on it, I was shot in my thigh, so he also tried to piece me up there. Then he was killed – right there beside me. To this day I still don't know who it was, but there was a third man who saved me. He dragged me back to the hedge line where we'd started. If it hadn't been for him, I would have died, too."

At the hedge line, Hotel Company Sgt. Jones heaved Sansosti into a fireman's carry and hauled him to safer ground. "He had an M-60 machine gun and he'd turn around every so often and pick off what he could." Finally, Jones got to a creek and put Sansosti onto a little boat. "We went down the creek and onto the Cua Viet River. I was helicoptered from there to the USS *Iwo Jima*, which had a small hospital. I was there for fifty-seven days, until I recovered. Then they sent me back to the bush in I Corps, which I was hoping wouldn't happen."

Sansosti holds two of his company's officers in highest regard: 2nd Lt. Baynard "Vic" Taylor (who assumed command after Capt. Williams was wounded) and Sgt. Jones, who carried Sansosti to safety. "Taylor had spent eight years as an enlisted man, returned to college and came back as our second lieutenant. He was very knowledgeable, as was Sgt. Jones. We would have followed them anywhere."

Aftermath of Dai Do

After three days of bloody fighting the cost was very high for both sides. The total American losses from April 30 to May 3 were: 3rd Marine Division, 233 killed, 821 wounded and one missing; the Navy, 15 killed and 22 wounded. ARVN (South Vietnamese) losses were recorded as 42 killed and 124 wounded. The NVA suffered an admitted 2,366 killed and an unknown number of wounded, with 43 POWs.

General Weise later reported, "Every Marine who was able to shoot, including wounded who could handle a weapon, fired and the fighting was violent and close. With the invaluable assistance of heavy naval fire, artillery and air assets, the NVA Division was finally forced back across the DMZ into North Vietnam. When the fighting of April 30 to May 3, 1968 was finished, there were two Medals of Honor, a Navy Cross and many other awards for heroism; and seemingly everyone had a Purple Heart." [Colin Heaton, *Vietnam Magazine*]

Medal of Honor *Navy Cross* *Purple Heart*

Many years later, General Weise met with the commander of the NVA 320th Division during a trip to Vietnam. During the conversation, the two battle commanders revealed that during the Battle of Dai Do, the Marines had no idea that they were up against a division of NVA, and the North Vietnamese didn't realize they were fighting just a handful of Marines.

The outcome of the Battle of Dai Do was extremely important to the U.S. war effort. The Marines' success prevented the NVA from destroying Marine headquarters at Dong Ha and its essential supplies of ammunition and fuel. Additionally, if the Americans had not prevailed at the Battle of Dai Do, many more American and South Vietnamese lives would have been lost in future attempts to retake the combat base at Dong Ha.

"The Marines who fought and died are affectionately called the Magnificent Bastards for good reason. Their performance, determination and dedication to their objective in the face of great numerical superiority were nothing less than magnificent." [Colin D. Heaton *Vietnam Magazine*]

Fifty Years Later

Sgt. Joe Sansosti was discharged in May 1970. He and his wife, Glenda, returned to western North Carolina where they enjoy a secluded forest view. On October 6, 2018, Sansosti was one of 92 Vietnam veterans on the Blue Ridge Honor Flight to Washington DC. The day's activities included an emotional visit to the Wall, where Sansosti found the names of his fallen comrades, especially Jerome Pryor. When the veterans returned, they were greeted by more than 1,000 cheering supporters. Sansosti noted the dramatic contrast with his flight home in 1968 when he couldn't get a seat on a plane. "It was very emotional. I had to fight back the tears."

Joe and Glenda Sansosti celebrated another significant anniversary in Quantico, Virginia, from April 30 to May 4, 2018 -- the 50th anniversary of the Battle of Dai Do and reunion of the 2nd Battalion 4th Marine Regiment and supporting forces. Sansosti met and spoke with Brig. Gen. William *Wild Bill* Weise, Maj. Gen. James Livingston, and Sansosti's Hotel Company Commander, Lt. Vic Taylor. It was a moving and gratifying experience. "Sgt. Jones didn't attend the reunion, which was disappointing because I wanted to thank him for carrying me out."

Maj. Gen. James Livingston, Joe Sansosti, and Brig. Gen. Wild Bill Weise at a Dai Do reunion.

In the anniversary book prepared for the reunion, Colin D. Heaton, author and a BLT 2/4 Marine, wrote the following:

> *To the American fighting men from all branches of the military who fought at Dai Do and in the Quang Tri operations during 1968, our nation owes you much. We also need to ensure that the legacy of this conflict is never omitted from our memory, nor can we forget the men who died serving our nation. Semper Fi!*

Lt. Vic Taylor and Joe, Quantico, May 2, 2018

MICHAEL D. KUHNE
A View from the Tonkin Gulf

*Ltjg Michael Kuhne in the Gulf of Tonkin
on USS Mahan DLG-11*

Michael Kuhne served in Vietnam on a ship in the Gulf of Tonkin from January through September 1970. His story is a series of reflections on his service, rather than a chronological account of events, and covers the period from his training at the U.S. Naval Academy through his tour in Vietnam.

I must tell you this before I begin my story: I never had to sleep in the rain, or in a swamp, or in a fox hole; I never had to be on point going down a trail in the jungle; I never had to carry a bleeding buddy to a medevac helo; and I never had to look into the eyes of the enemy's casualties.

How did I get to Vietnam? My mom and dad were in the WWII European theater. To my dad, like so many other dads on our block and in our town, patriotism was a given. There was a sacred commitment to defend our nation and the hopes of others around the world. Trips to the Air Force Academy to see football games and hear concerts convinced me that such a path of service should be mine. I must admit that the uniforms, hot cars and stunning girls that were part of the cadets' aura had an influential impact on me! But instead of the Air Force Academy, I received an appointment to the Naval Academy in 1966. (I think their uniforms were most handsome.)

At the Academy, Vietnam was ever-present in our minds. We observed a tradition of silence in our mess hall and the ringing of the bell when it was reported that another of our alumni had been killed in Vietnam. As the four years progressed, we recognized the names of our upper classmen. Our Memorial Hall had photos of those men and as the years passed, more photos were posted. These sad moments did not dampen our commitment and willingness to sacrifice for "a cause greater than oneself." As a matter of fact, as peace talks sputtered, many of us were concerned that the war would end without our individual contribution.

We studied history and recognized the brutality of the dictatorships of Hitler, Stalin, and Mao, and we believed our cause was noble and just. But not all concurred outside the walls of the Academy. With the battles of Hue and Khe Sanh, the Tet Offensive, and the draft, many in the public damned us. I recall how our Brigade of Midshipmen would march to the stadium for a football game on a Saturday and college students from a nearby campus would jeer and spit. I have had decades now to reflect upon that behavior and the rationale some used in protesting and in doing everything to avoid and evade the conflict in Vietnam. These reflections are another story.

"So, what did you do in the war, Daddy?"

I was stationed on the USS *Mahan* (DLG-11), a guided missile frigate responsible for directing aircraft from carriers onto targets in North Vietnam and providing anti-aircraft protection to the task force and shore bombardment. Our station was in the Gulf of Tonkin, north of Yankee Station, across from Hainan Island and close to Haiphong.

USS Mahan, Guided Missile Frigate

We had a "spook shack" on the fantail for a few weeks. Navy cryptologists and other spooky dudes manned this box and monitored enemy radio traffic. With the mining of Haiphong Harbor, Soviet ships attempting to bring armaments to the North Vietnamese Army (NVA), and China's support of the Ho Chi Minh regime, our spooks performed a wide array of monitoring.

Sleep was elusive since underway replenishment for fuel, food and ammo occurred every other night in addition to 12-hour watches. Typically, we would average two-to-four hours' sleep during these intense periods which came far too frequently.

The USS *Worden* relieved us as we went to Sattahip, Thailand, for R&R, spending only one day in Bangkok before being recalled back to the ship. The *Worden* had been hit with missiles resulting in deadly casualties. We took our station again, now aware that North Vietnam torpedo boats or MIGS were actively attacking our ships. (Later the investigation revealed it to be a "friendly fire" situation where fighter escorts for B-52 bombers sent a missile to the origin of a radiating and locked-on radar, *Worden* being the source.).

Comrades in Arms

I was privileged to fly with a classmate as he flew the *Big Mother*, a search-and-rescue helo that was armored, packing a Gatling gun-type of weapon. Although for me this was a joy ride, he flew many heroic and harrowing missions into enemy territory.

One of my classmates, a fighter pilot, attended a briefing by the air wing. Amidst the bravado he always exhibited, there was now a focus and seriousness that reflected this was not a joy ride. The numbers of POWs, KIAs and MIAs from that naval aviation branch were a testimony to the seriousness of each mission.

During a repair visit in Subic Bay in the Philippines, I ran into a SEAL we had worked with doing insertions from a submarine in the islands off San Diego. He reminded me that those practice sessions had resulted in successful operations in recent months. I still am in awe of those amazing warriors.

Aboard the USS *Mahan* in the Tonkin Gulf

Shipmates aboard the USS Mahan. Kuhne is standing, 3rd from the left.

The bell tower of a church in Quang Tri near the demilitarized zone (DMZ) was intact on a Sunday morning, despite an endless line of ships firing upon that target. I witnessed every form of military power exerted on that piece of Vietnam, including B-52's, F-4's, A-4's and A-6's, attack helos and intense bombardment from battleships and destroyers. What were we determined to destroy? I still don't know. Perhaps that is the sad reality: when destruction is so far off, we cannot see what harm we have caused.

Standing on the bridge of the USS *Mahan*, looking out and seeing an armada across the Gulf that was reminiscent of those photos of the fleet during WWII, stunned me. During our deployment, there were five carriers in the Gulf at the same time. Hundreds of airstrikes occurred daily and watching those aircraft take off and land over and over again on that postage stamp deck of a carrier was a sight to behold.

But of all my moments in the Gulf, one incident still haunts me. One black night, with all ships in a darkened condition (no navigational lights), a catastrophe of huge proportions was averted. Radar indicated *constant bearing, decreasing range* (collision imminent). No matter which way I turned, it seemed the other vessel changed course to continue this perilous outcome. Only by the grace of God, did I order shift rudder at the last moment to avoid a collision that would have resulted in numerous deaths. Seeing the dark profile of that other vessel pass quickly across my bow, I realized how close we were to tragedy.

Silence aboard the USS Mahan

I never had to notify family members of the ultimate sacrifice their loved one made. But on that dark night, I discovered that a 24-year-old Ltjg is truly responsible for hundreds of lives.

These few thoughts come to my mind when I contemplate the uniqueness of the situation and circumstances of my time in the Gulf of Tonkin. They are not spectacular when compared to others' stories, told by those who faced the rage and horrors of war. I thank those who did so much beyond what I did. I pray that the hauntings that some encounter will leave them. I know that "there but for the grace of God, go I."

Reunion, Loss and Reflections

In 1973, after the U.S. departure from Vietnam, I was an instructor at the Naval Amphibious Base in Coronado, teaching a counterinsurgency curriculum. We hosted 27 Cambodian naval officers in San Diego. As part of the alliance with Lon Nol, this strategy-planning program was beneficial for both groups; but seeing their wonderment at Disneyland was a delight. Within a year after their return, we learned that all had been killed in the purges of Pol Pot and his Khmer Rouge. The brutality of dictatorships had not been blunted.

Having visited the battlefields where my grandfather and my dad fought, I revel in their heroism. Although I hear the accolades given to their generations, always followed by "we don't have such anymore," I protest. For during my brief time in the military, I saw in my shipmates a dedication to service. It was a unique focus and brotherhood. I was also blessed to see the heroism of those who flew the rescue missions, the special forces who took on dangerous challenges and those who survived the horrors of the jungle.

Hearing the emotional reflections by men who were at Khe Sanh, the Mekong River, and dozens of other hell-holes makes me realize that the blood of my father and grandfather, and all those dads of my youth, does flow in the veins of these amazing warriors and will continue as our country requires.

And to my mom, Lt. Nola Belle O'Connor Kuhne, a WWII Army nurse in the European theater, I salute you, for many more brave women now follow and stand in the forefront of those who willingly accept that their sacrifice could be ultimate.

Mike's mother: Lt. Nola Belle O'Connor Kuhne, Army Nurse, Operation Torch

Mike Kuhne, 2019

John "Larry" McCall
Securing the Mekong Delta

*9th Infantry Division
shoulder insignia*

Self-proclaimed Carolina mountain boy John "Larry" McCall was drafted into the Army in 1968 at age 19. McCall's father had provided a compelling example of answering the call of duty. An Air Force navigator during WWII, he spent two years as a German prisoner of war. "Although he died when we were very young, he was still a major influence in our lives."

Larry and nine other young men from his North Carolina mountain community reported to Fort Bragg for basic training and then to Fort Polk, Louisiana, for Advanced Infantry Training. To his regret, upon their arrival in Vietnam, his nine friends were dispersed to the 25th Infantry Division in the jungle, while he was sent to the 9th Infantry Division, in Tân Tru and Tân An, southwest of Saigon. Nicknamed the *Old Reliables* during WWII, the 9th Infantry Division served with the Mobile Riverine Force in Vietnam's fertile Mekong Delta, a vast maze of rice paddies broken up by rivers, swamps, narrow canals and dikes. Their mission was to secure this extremely challenging battleground against the Viet Cong Communist insurgents. During the Vietnam War the delta was the site of many Army search-and-destroy missions.

Fighting in the Mekong Delta

"Our base camp consisted of a tent with a wooden platform. We travelled primarily by helicopter which dropped us into the flooded rice paddies." The U.S. objective was to initiate battles with the Viet Cong and use the Army's superior firepower to inflict large losses. "We would be out there anywhere from two-to-three weeks before they'd return to pick us up, so we had to watch our rations and ammunition supplies very carefully. Sometimes we had to walk back to our base camp.

"The helicopters didn't have any doors, so everything was open. At first, for a little old mountain boy like me, if it had been possible, I would have jumped out. It scared me so much, but after a while I got used to it." The delta's climate was an additional impediment during McCall's early days in Vietnam. "I was evacuated from the field for heat exhaustion twice. Eventually my system adjusted to the extremely hot, humid climate and I didn't have any more trouble."

McCall once leapt from a helicopter which had been hit. "It was spinning, so we jumped out of it. Luckily, we were over the rice paddies. We never hit solid ground. Sometimes it was chest deep. We had to wiggle our way out of the water and mud, watching for snakes and leeches." The checkerboard of rice paddies was separated by dikes of mounded dirt used to navigate the area. "We always walked in the rice paddies. We never walked on the dikes because they were booby-trapped. It wasn't an easy life."

During one battle, McCall rescued a first lieutenant whose helicopter had been shot down, for which he received a Bronze Star. "We were family over there. We didn't try to get familiar because we might not be there very long, but we always helped each other as much as possible."

In February 1969, during the Tet Offensive, McCall was shot in the arm and leg. After a week in a Saigon hospital he was flown to Tokyo where they reopened his wounds and sewed him back up. Given the option of returning to his unit or going home, he chose home and returned to Fort Bragg where he

Larry McCall receiving his Purple Heart while in the hospital.

received therapy for his arm and leg. McCall completed his active duty at Fort Bragg and received an honorable discharge.

Coming Home: Challenges and the Effects of Agent Orange

Back home, protestors, accustomed to viewing disturbing images and updated body counts on the nightly news, vented their frustration with the government's policies on returning soldiers. Coming through the San Diego airport in uniform, Sergeant First Class Larry McCall endured verbal abuse and insolent treatment from many of his countrymen. "They called me a pot-head, among other things. I was around the stuff over there, but I didn't use it. I had other things on my mind. I couldn't understand why they were so negative about us. We were asked to go, and we went. And when we came back, they looked at us as if we weren't human beings. Today people come up to me and say, 'thank you.' It feels good, but I wonder where they were 50 years ago."

Elaine & Larry on their wedding day, Dec. 1, 1969

Football team captain Larry and homecoming queen and valedictorian Elaine had been high school sweethearts. Elaine was a college student when Larry left for Vietnam and remembers similarly rude behavior on her campus. "We were engaged before Larry left, and I was a student at Asheville/Buncombe Technical College. I was in the student union when a guy sitting near me asked, 'Why do you want to be engaged to somebody who's going to come home with no arms or legs?' I was so shocked, I slapped him in the face. I assumed I'd be in big trouble, but the teacher in my next class said to me, 'Good for you!' The whole thing was out of character for me, but that fellow never said anything ugly to me again."

Like many Vietnam veterans, McCall suffered from PTSD. After arriving in the states, he was met by his family at a bus station at Fort Bragg. His fiancée, Elaine, came up behind him to give him a welcoming hug. "My first instinct was to knock her away because of what I'd been through." Elaine has her own story to tell. "One day, several years after he got back, a helicopter flew over our house while we were sleeping. He woke up and was frantic. He said, 'Where am I?' The helicopter sounds really scared him."

The most lasting effects of McCall's tour in Vietnam are serious health issues related to the toxic defoliant, Agent Orange. "We recognized the areas that had been sprayed because they looked like somebody had burned everything around, and there was a big fog. They brought in the planes and sprayed the soldiers in the field along with the vegetation. We didn't know exactly what it was, until we came stateside and started having health issues. I couldn't eat anything. I almost died." McCall suffered a heart attack and pancreatitis with resultant diabetes. "I only have one-third of my pancreas." Recently a specialist at the VA Hospital found a way to bypass McCall's pancreas. "He saved my life."

Back in the Mountains

Although reluctant to make the trip, Larry visited the Vietnam Veterans Memorial after years of urging by his wife, Elaine, and daughter, Andrea. "I located the names of my friends on the wall. I saw family members making rubbings of their loved ones' names, and leaving behind flowers, flags, and other mementos. It was very moving for everyone. I think it's a great memorial."

After leaving the Army, McCall worked for the postal service, carrying mail for many years. He married Elaine and the couple have a son, Jonathan, and their daughter, Andrea. Now a Deacon at his church, McCall divides his time between volunteering at church and travelling with his family. After Vietnam's rice paddies, Italy, France, and Hawaii hold a special charm for this man of the mountains.

Larry and Elaine McCall, 2018

SGT. 1ST CLASS CURTISS L. POTEAT, USA (RET.)
Patrolling the Rivers of South Vietnam

Poteat with AK-47 at his base in Cat Lai

Private Curtiss L. "Chris" Poteat left the tranquility of Marion, NC, for South Vietnam in 1969, having trained as a Military Policeman to work on Army Patrol Boats (PBRs). "When I graduated from high school, my draft number was three, so I went ahead and joined the Army. The uncle I'm named after was on PT boats in WWII, and I liked McHale's Navy, so I thought that river boats would be a cool job."

Providing River Security

South Vietnam, especially the Mekong Delta area in the south, is marked by numerous waterways presenting serious logistical obstacles to U.S. ground forces. To resolve this problem, the Navy created the Mobile Riverine Force -- a partnership between the Army and Navy in fighting the war in the rice paddies, canals, and treacherous waterways of the south.

Poteat was assigned to the 18th MP Brigade as a member of the *458 Sea Tigers*. The Sea Tigers, initially cargo handlers, evolved into warriors. With the addition of 50 caliber machine guns, M60 machine guns, automatic grenade launchers, and personal weapons, these boats provided essential water-borne security for river operations.

Poteat at Cat Lai

Poteat's cousin was an MP at firebase Bastogne.

"All the security in Vietnam was under the 18th MP Brigade, including the PBRs. My job as an MP was to maintain the weapons. If we didn't shoot them, I just oiled them and pulled covers over them; but if they'd been fired, I carried the 50's up to 55-gallon drums of acetone and cleaned them. Then I reassembled them and mounted them on the boat. I had to breathe all that acetone. My skin turned chalky white and peeled off.

"They sent me down to a little place called Cat Lai where we provided security for a SEAL team detachment, dropping them off somewhere on the river, ready to extract them or provide cover fire if necessary. The SEALs went out on a boat called a Boston Whaler, which is like a little fishing boat. It could maneuver into shallower water, touching shore so they could get out. We were well-armed and stood ready to provide support if they were ambushed."

Patrol river boat PBR

Security for large fuel and ammo ships also fell to Poteat's unit. Viet Cong *sappers* (commandos), often invisible wearing divers' tanks and masks, would attempt to place limpet (magnetic) mines on the bottom of ships to blow holes in them. "We spent all night circling the ships, dropping concussion grenades in the water and sometimes bringing up bodies. The Viet Cong had been fighting for a long time -- the French, the Japanese, the French again, and now the Americans. They knew what they were doing. They were our friends during the day and our enemy at night."

Finding a Mole

"During the Tet Offensive in 1970, the Viet Cong attacked the wire around our base and set off our booby traps and flares. We called in the Navy Seawolves (armed helicopters), and the Viet Cong were repelled by the gunships and by our security boats on the river. The next day we pulled nearly 140 bodies out of the wire. One of them was our camp barber, a VC mole who had been sending strategic information to the enemy."

Repelling an Ambush

Poteat and a driver from his unit were transporting two engines to their PBRs in Vung Tau in a five-ton truck when they came upon a convoy of 25 vehicles which had been ambushed. "The VC had blown the first and last vehicles which trapped the convoy. They fired on us. We had two M16s and an M60 mounted on a ring on top of the truck, so I stood on the ring and opened up on the machine gun. We busted the ambush. A captain from the convoy got our names and thanked us, giving us each a bottle of Vietnamese beer. All in all, we thought we'd come out ahead."

Silver &Bronze Stars

To his surprise, 18 months later back home at Fort Bragg, Poteat was awarded the Silver Star for his service on the road to Vung Tau. At the same time, he received the Bronze Star with a V for Valor, awarded for the night his compound was attacked. He takes no credit for bravery, stating that he did what had to be done to stay alive.

No C-Rats Tonight!

In a letter home, Curtiss told his mother that he missed her spaghetti dinners. One night, as he and his unit prepared for a dinner of combat rations, he received a large box from his mother, delivered with the mail by helicopter. "I thought, 'what the heck is this and how can I carry it out here in the bush?' Inside were four boxes of spaghetti noodles, four large cans of Chef Boyardee spaghetti sauce, two cans of B&B mushrooms and two cans of parmesan cheese."

The resourceful soldiers used their k-bars to make forks from their spoons. After removing the liners, they filled their helmets with water from the nearby river, using them to cook the noodles, and heated the sauce in machine gun ammo cans. "Everyone else had c-rats and sniffed the air because they smelled spaghetti. We dined in style. One of our guys said, 'You thought of everything! This even has oregano in it.' I said, 'Dumb ass, that's the paint from inside your helmet.'"

Home and Back to 'Nam

Curtiss returned to the states on leave in September 1971, flying into Elmendorf AFB in Alaska. "When we left Vietnam, it was 120 degrees and we were wearing jungle fatigues. We landed at Elmendorf at 2 a.m. and it was minus 10 degrees. We had to deplane to transfer to a different aircraft. We tried get in, but the doors were locked. We were ready to break the door down when they finally let us in. Then on to Oakland. It took us a day-and-a-half to get there. I went home on two-week leave, but my fiancé was marrying somebody else and I wasn't fitting in well at home. So I called Fort Bragg and they sent me orders to return to Vietnam. I went back after one week.

"When I returned, we'd turned our boats over to the Vietnamese in July, so I was back to being an MP on convoys. I worked as an advisor to the 9th Army Division on weapons and stayed with them until the end of May of 1972. One good thing I'll say about Vietnam, it's a beautiful country. And I liked a lot of the food. I never asked what the meat was. The joke was that it might be somebody you knew or petted."

In May 1972, Sergeant Curtiss Poteat left Vietnam for good and tried attending college, but the anti-war sentiment on campus disturbed him. "I fought with the protesters. I couldn't understand people protesting something they weren't involved in. They worried about people being killed; I was fired on every day and who worried about me?"

Artifacts and Vietnam History

In a distinctive room in the Veterans History Museum of the Carolinas in Brevard, NC, visitors encounter a remarkable display of military artifacts depicting life during the Vietnam War. Many noteworthy items were donated by Curtiss, including uniforms, c-rations, a Viet Cong hammock, a North Vietnamese flag, radios, and weapons. How did he acquire these mementos and get them back to the United States? "I took several items, including a hammock and a North Vietnamese flag, off a sampan which had fired on us and which we seized. During the Tet Offensive, when the Viet Cong attacked the wire around our base, I was on the bow of a river boat, manning the 50-caliber machine guns. An RPG-40 (grenade) hit the gunnel, punched through the edge of the boat, and exploded, sending shrapnel down on my shoulders and other body parts. While I was in the hospital, knowing I'd be there for a while, I called my cousin and asked him to bring my belongings from Cat Lai to the hospital. I meant my personal letters and the contents in my locker. Well, he crammed everything which was near my bunk into a duffel bag. I just sent it all home."

Curtiss Poteat, posing with some of the artifacts sent home from Vietnam, including uniforms, flags, and C-rats.

Curtiss re-enlisted in the Army, serving his country until his retirement as a Sergeant First Class in October 1992. He and his wife, Jean, reside in Mills River, NC. He holds his comrades in highest regard. "My heroes never wore football or basketball or baseball jerseys. My heroes wore uniforms. The did something meaningful for our country, not just for themselves."

Welcome Home, Brother

Louis P. "Phil" Mayrand, Jr.
Army Ranger Recounts His Last Mission in Vietnam

75th Ranger Regiment insignia

Phil Mayrand's account, in his own words, of his last mission in Vietnam.

On the morning of August 5, 1969, Ranger Sergeant Joe Little, Team Leader and I, Assistant Team Leader, received the warning order for Ranger Team 2-1's next mission. We were to go in heavy with an atypically large team of eight Rangers to be inserted on the west bank of the Vam Co Dong River at the Parrot's Beak. The location was just east of the Cambodian border, about three miles from a 5,000-man strong North Vietnamese Army compound. That afternoon Sgt. Little and I were flown over the insertion site by helicopter to survey the site, since our night insertion would have poor-to-no visibility. This section of the river was dubbed *blood alley* by the U.S. Navy's Brown Water Navy due to the highest level of combat contact for the Riverine forces of PBRs (Patrol Boat River), Monitors, and Swift Boats during the Vietnam War.

Insertion into Blood Alley

We were inserted by two Navy PBRs in the very early hours of August 6, under the cover of darkness. The designated position for our observation post and ambush position had been flooded, so we moved back close to the river and set up in an artillery shell crater. After daylight, the team was discovered by a Vietnamese woman and child (likely an enemy sympathizer) who came to set up a fishing net on the riverbank just below our position. Having been compromised, we radioed the tactical operations center at Co. F, 75th Rangers in Chu Chi and requested extraction several times that day. We were denied and advised to continue the mission.

Just before nightfall, I was monitoring the radio on the 25th Inf. Div. aviation frequency. The pilot of the helicopter gunship said he was breaking contact with enemy personnel because of his proximity to our team. As it became completely dark, we could hear voices and the enemy crashing through the vegetation as they neared our position. Team Leader Joe Little quietly spread the word to prepare for contact and to wait to blow our claymore mines until he set off the lead claymore.

At the same time, another Ranger team from our small contingent of temporary duty Rangers assigned to the tiny, remote Navy base of Tra Cu, was being inserted nearby on the opposite bank of the river. We did not blow our flank claymores (toward river) so as not to endanger the other Rangers and Navy Riverine personnel. Instructions on the back of claymore mines caution users to stay back 100 meters to prevent back-blast injury. Our claymores were 5 meters outside our position. On signal, we detonated them. When a dozen or so claymores go off almost simultaneously in such proximity, it sounds and feels like the end of the world.

Our standard operating procedure after initial contact for all team members was to put out twenty minutes of devastating small arms fire (M-60 machine gun, M-40 grenade launcher, 28mm grenades, M-16 rifles, CAR 15's, etc.). Ranger Sgt. Bob Newsom fired his M-60 machine gun to the extent that it warped the barrel. I fired about 20 magazines of ammo with my M-16 until it was too hot to hold, even with my olive drab towel wrapped around it. Hot brass from expended rounds was flying everywhere. The noise of the remaining six weapons being fired was deafening beyond belief.

"Everyone was hit."

Suddenly, there was a high flash followed by a double explosion. I was up on my knees firing my weapon and was blown to the left. My head was driven into the muddy bank of the artillery crater. Immediately, ears ringing and caked with mud, I crawled to my rucksack and PRC-25 radio and raised the tactical operations center. The Co. F Executive Officer, 1st. Lt. Tomaschek, asked how badly we were hit. I reported that we were hit bad, but I needed illumination to give an accurate situation report. As soon as the artillery battery assigned to us had illumination up, the Navy patrol boats engaged the sappers that hit us. They had lobbed their satchel charge into our position as they ran along the edge of the river. The satchel charge landed between Ranger Sargent John F. Crikelair and Ranger Specialist 4th Class Earnest Heard and detonated some of our own ordnance. Sadly, they both died later that night at the 12th Evacuation Hospital at Chu Chi.

The team was devastated; everyone was hit. Sergeant Little was hit the worst of the surviving six Rangers. His wounds rendered him incapable of continuing to command Ranger Team 2-1; therefore, the fate of our team was in my hands. In keeping with the Ranger Creed, and with the cooperation of the Navy and Army medevac helicopters, we made sure no man was left behind. After the Navy moved us across river to a more suitable medevac landing zone, the other Ranger Team went to our former position to retrieve gear. They found several blood trails of enemy, but no bodies.

Mayrand in ambush position during a mission

We believe there had been a division-level decision not to extract but to leave us as bait to draw out the North Vietnamese Army in the nearby compound.

Sgt. Little, Sgt. Newsom, and I were evacuated to a huge U.S. military hospital in Yokohama, Japan, to recover. Both Little and Newsom were sent back to military hospitals in the U.S. Unfortunately, Newson succumbed to Agent Orange cancer in 2012.

I stayed at the medevac hospital in Yokohama for two months to recover. I was reassigned to Korat, Thailand, for the remainder of my time overseas (I was in Vietnam less than three months). The remaining Team 2-1 members recovered from their wounds in-country and at least two eventually resumed back-to-back three-day four-night Long Range Patrol missions.

"Welcome to Company F"

How does a relatively small (5'8", 155 lbs.) college student end up in the Long-Range Patrol (Airborne Rangers) with the elite 75th Rangers in Vietnam? During the early-to-mid-20th century, the Charles Atlas Workout Program promised transformation from the skinny kid who had sand kicked in his face by bullies on the beach into a tough guy that could effectively protect himself and his girlfriend. In the spring of 1964, before I graduated from Reynolds High in Winston-Salem, I was that proverbial skinny kid. My pal Charlie and I decided not to take it anymore, so we met with the U.S. Army recruiter, hoping to become Airborne Ranger Green Berets. One day the recruiter called my home to speak to me, but my father answered. I was told in no uncertain terms that I was going to college that fall.

Four years later, I was drafted out of college just before I was to finish an Associate of Science in Civil Engineering, but was able to talk my draft board into letting me finish my A.S. before being inducted into the Army.

This was occurring just after the Tet Offensive. The evening news was full of Vietnam and stories about war protesters. I was in love with my college sweetheart and decided to volunteer for the draft to get my enlistment over in two years. I wanted to be with her sooner rather than the three or four-year commitment from other regular military units. I really had few choices as I was 1A and could not get a job. I naively thought that since I had an A.S. in Civil Engineering, the worst thing that could happen to me would be to end up as a combat engineer.

AIT Fort Polk, triple bad luck!

In basic training the scuttlebutt was that at the end of training, the worst military occupational skill you could be assigned was 11B -- small arms infantry. If you were unfortunate enough to get 11B, the worst training base for AIT (Advanced Infantry Training) was Fort Polk, Louisiana, but at least you'd get a short leave before you had to report for training. However, I had tested so poorly as I entered the Army that I ended as 11B, at Ft. Polk with no leave. Triple bad luck!

Mayrand holding a CAR-15 & LAW

While I was at Ft. Polk, I tried to get out of 11B. I was stuck with that assignment, so I volunteered to go to infantry Non-Commissioned Officer Candidate School (NCOCS). This would allow me the training and rank I desired and could be accomplished within the two-year enlistment. At the end of NCOCS, we had a choice: complete our training by returning to AIT and serving as a platoon sergeant through a training cycle; or, go to Ranger School. I chose Ranger training because I knew I was headed for combat in Vietnam and I wanted the best possible training.

In Vietnam, I was shipped to Chu Chi, home of the 25th Infantry Division, aka *The Electric Strawberry* or officially *Tropic Lightning*. I was terrified, (I admit I was terrified the entire time I was in-country), as I had no idea to whom I would be assigned. As soon as I got to Chu Chi, I was sent to a transient detachment to await assignment. I was so worried that I went to the base chapel to pray for the best assignment possible. As I was walking back into the transient detachment area, someone called my name and I was told to grab my gear as I was shipping. There was a jeep waiting for me, and shortly we pulled up in front of a company area with a sign that said, Co. F 75th Infantry Airborne Ranger.

When I reported to the commanding officer, he apprised me that he had volunteered me for company F, having seen on my personnel file that I was 11B4G MOS (small arms infantry airborne Ranger NCO). In effect he told me "If you don't want us, we don't want you. You have to want to be in the Long-Range Patrol." He requested that I remain with Co. F for at least two weeks and go out on at least one mission before deciding whether I wanted to stay. He told me that if I did not choose to stay with Co. F, he would see that I got the best assignment possible.

The commanding officer made it clear that if I chose to stay, he could guarantee two results: first, I would complete standard three-day four-night missions back-to-back for

11 1/2 months (if I survived); and second, I would receive the Purple Heart as we had 90% casualties. "Welcome to Co. F, Sgt. Mayrand." I chose to stay. Despite these statistics, the 75th Infantry Rangers had very high morale and esprit de corps as an elite fighting team. We were truly brothers who loved each other.

The 75th Infantry had 13 companies in Vietnam, each assigned to a major infantry division as the on the ground division-level intelligence group. At the time I was there, our mission was to monitor and report enemy troop movements, engaging them in combat whenever possible. When we were inserted on these missions, our faces and all exposed skin were painted with camouflage. Everything was silenced for stealthy insertions. Because our tactics were extremely effective, we had targets on our backs. If the enemy troops could bring back proof of having killed a Ranger, they were set for life, with something like a $2,500 bounty – a veritable fortune in those days for the Vietnamese. We were expensive bait.

What am I proud of about my service? I am proud of the people I served with. I am proud of the training I received and credit my survival and that of others on Ranger Team 2-1 to having attended Ranger School. Finally, I am proud I was able to execute my duties when the #@*% hit the fan. The war, not so much.

Phil and Diane Mayrand at a Ranger reunion

Mayrand's awards and decorations include: Silver Star, Purple Heart, Combat Infantry Badge, Ranger Tab, Vietnam Service Medal with three Bronze Service Stars, Republic of Vietnam Gallantry Cross Unit Citation, Vietnam Civil Actions Honor Medal Unit Citation, National Defense Medal, Good Conduct Medal, Expert Marksmanship Badge with Machinegun bar, Sharpshooter Marksmanship badge with Rifle Bar, and Marksmanship Badge, with Auto Rifle Bar.

Lt. Col. C. G. "Jug" Gerard, USMC (Ret.)

From Jet Jockey to Helicopters

Marine Observation Squadron 6 "Tomcats"

Jug Gerard's account, in his own words, of his missions as a USMC helicopter pilot.

I had a fulfilling diverse twenty-five-year Marine Corps career, from 1956 as a Naval Aviation cadet in Pensacola to the final years as teaching faculty at the Armed Forces Staff College in Norfolk, Virginia. My initial goal was to become a Marine jet pilot. To that end, I was successful. However, at the end of three years of A-4C jet attack squadron flying in spring of 1963, I received a shock – orders to helicopter transition training.

Marine planners were aware of probable Vietnam involvement. New turbine-jet engine helicopters were also on order to replace the venerable reciprocating-engine predecessors. With that threat and the new inventory, more seats would have to be filled. Five hundred fifty fixed-wing pilots were dragged 'kicking and screaming' into the transition program. Transition training was in the old reliable UH-34D. Six weeks later, I was what jet pilots reflected on at the time as second-class citizens: a helicopter pilot.

Observation Squadron and the UH-1E Huey Helicopter

Orders then put me in a unique one-of-a-kind observation squadron (VMO-1). The squadron was flying two antiquated aircraft, the fixed-wing 0-1 Bird Dog airplane and the wooden rotor blade wonder-machine, the UH-43D helicopter. My preference was the reliable Bird Dog, which I flew for 450 hours. I received minimal instruction in the cantankerous UH-43D before the arrival of the all-new turbine jet Huey.

My introductory flight was April 2, 1964, in the Marine Corps' first turbo-jet engine helicopter. During the following three years, I honed skills with the Huey, along with monitoring the ever-expanding inventory of new helicopters entering service.

Upon arrival in Vietnam on September 1, 1967, I was assigned to VMO-6, a squadron of friends and familiar faces from years stateside. The next 13 months were regarded as the most active period of the war. As a new major with the most Huey hours in the Corps, I was immediately positioned to lead. During the month of September, as a new guy, I flew 100 hours of first-pilot combat time, which set the pattern for the next six months. Fortunately, good Marine training prepared us for what was encountered and Marine helicopter performance in Vietnam was exemplary.

The Huey as a Gunship

The VMO (observation squadron) mission changed from the introduction 3 ½ years prior. In addition to traditional squadron missions, the Huey was now a gunship with four forward-firing machine guns and two seven-shot 2.75-inch rocket pods plus two crew-man side firing guns. We were closely tied to the CH-46 transport squadrons that took the true brunt of hardship and heroics in the Marine Vietnam helicopter flying. With our guns, we often escorted them on their missions. The enemy learned to bypass our armed gunships and wait for the less-defended transports, but the odds were greatly improved when we were there.

The most satisfying observation missions were Forward Air Controller (AIRBORNE). We were the intermediary between the Marines on the ground needing heavy ordnance and the jets that could provide it. We had dual-frequency radios to allow transmission to both parties and the ability to get low and slow to positively identify with white phosphorus rockets the exact location mud-Marines deemed needing attention and then guiding the jets to the specific spot. On many occasions, I found I was directing former squadron mates from jet days onto those ground targets – always an appreciated encounter.

Major C.G. "Jug" Gerard, Vietnam 1967

Working with Marine Reconnaissance Teams

We also had close ties with Marine Reconnaissance Teams. Recon was the eyes and ears in the field always seeking the enemy and any evasive spot they might otherwise be clandestinely working, most often in the jungle. Inserting those teams via transport helicopter always proved interesting and pulling them out, usually under emergency conditions, was tense and challenging. The gunship escorts always attended and were often in control of jet-provided ordnance when extractions went bad.

Our home base moved north in 1967 until we were at an airfield at Quang Tri, 15 miles south of the DMZ. It assuredly is where the action was. From that point, in addition to conventional missions, the transport and observation squadron became the sole helicopter support for the combat base at Khe Sanh. All supply support came from the air, for Highway 9 was severed. A decision made in late 1967 would keep two Hueys and two CH-46s continually at Khe Sanh to reduce response times for on-call requirements.

Gunship Escort and Reconnaissance at Khe Sanh

VMO-6 would take the commitment in two-week stands. I was to take the first detachment beginning January 1, 1968. The combat base was the site of a major battle in spring 1967 fought on rather conventional terms until the North withdrew. Although the base was now relatively quiet, it stuck out to the northwest, constantly inviting attention from the North Vietnamese. I visited the base on single-day support flights but knew little about the facility or the threat. These first two weeks, and the following three months of 1968, provided ample time to learn the working of Khe Sanh.

Col. David Lownds, Commander of the 26th Marines, was the base commander. His headquarters was in the old French fort, a structure built by the French in pentagon configuration of thick brick walls buried two-thirds below the surrounding ground level. The base was bare-bones functional. A 3,000-foot east-west Marston-mat runway had a distinct uphill grade toward hills to the west and a precipitous drop off the eastern end. Helicopters parked in a six-plane revetment complex that provided maximum protection from incoming ordnance. Every conceivable military function was available in base support. It was encircled with triple-roll concertina wire with trench lines and strategic gun emplacements. The red clay carried with it a crimson imprint for everything touched. Initially we were in the dry season; soon when all was rain and fog, it was gumbo.

Our conventional wood frame and plywood Southeast Asia hooch, with metal frame racks and mattresses, was every bit as good as our Quang Tri accommodations. The eight-man detachment fit comfortably. Nights were cool, so we slept under poncho liners. A sandbag bunker for protection behind the building was a constant reminder that hostile fire was probable.

In addition to gunship escort for the transport helicopters providing daily support to the surrounding hill outposts, we delved heavily into reconnaissance. Daily we flew intelligence-gathering flights into all quadrants. We were a small input to the greater intelligence-gathering effort for what was developing around Khe Sanh. The enemy was out there and only the number and intent were undetermined. Our efforts did uncover extraordinary sightings, but we were never allowed to act upon them, just report.

Spotting Caves and Elephants

To the west, along the single-track dirt road, misleadingly labeled Highway 9, was a lush green Lang Vei coffee plantation, next to an Army Special Forces compound also identified as Lang Vei. Just beyond the border with Laos stood the opposing vertical face of Co Rock Mountain. Pocketed within its face were numerous caves – some camouflaged, but there was enough exposure that we counted barrels of artillery pieces unquestionably pointed at Khe Sanh proper, 20 miles to the east. We could see the weapons, but not the personnel who always remained out of sight. We were directed not to cross into Laos.

One day, south of Lang Vei beyond a low-running ridge, we found a large grass meadow which revealed tire tracks from vehicle activities. More surprising, browsing under broad-limbed trees were four dusty elephants. Painted on their sides were large identifying colored numerals. It was unquestionably significant, but what do we do with something of that kind?

The "People Sniffer"

VMO-6 was a custodian to an equipment item dubbed *People Sniffer*, which mounted a wand under the Huey for gathering air samples and a sensing unit in the cabin for processing. When flown at low altitudes and slow air speeds over the landscape, it had the capability of "sniffing" and chemically testing the air for human urine. Supposedly, it classified monkey urine the same as human urine, but no other species could confound the equipment. The Sniffer was highly classified and only several squadron pilots were trained on the operation to obtain maximum reliable reading. One afternoon, squadron commander Col. White came to Khe Sanh to spend a full afternoon to sniff the valleys and hills around the base that our previous searching identified as probably "hot." I flew about 1,000 feet above his low-level flight path with a map on which we placed an X over every point he called off as giving a significant reading. The Sniffer report revealed there was a huge human urine trace throughout the area – either people or it was an equally significant number of monkeys. The bottom line helped support the fact that a hostile buildup was growing around Khe Sanh.

My group was replaced January 14 by Dave Workman's group. At O-dark-thirty the morning of January 22, Workman's group awakened along with everyone else to the initial all-out attack on the combat base. The "Siege of Khe Sanh" had begun. Over the next three months, I returned to Khe Sanh almost daily for control of jets, overnight on-call standby, or escort for CH-46 transport.

The siege continued until April 15 when the Army formally moved into the area and relieved the 26th Marines of control. Highway 9 opened again to vehicle traffic and the whole complexion of the contested area changed. The NVA had withdrawn after horrendous losses. The surrounding countryside was as pockmarked as the surface of the moon with bomb craters.

Returning Home

Upon my return to continental U.S. through San Francisco September 1968, I had sobering exposure to unbridled anti-Vietnam mentality. Long hair, loud, weird casual clothing leaning to bell-bottoms and peacenik t-shirts, along with braless women were prominent at the airport. I was travelling in uniform, which prompted stares, finger-pointing and hisses. A shave in the terminal barbershop from an anti-war advocate with a straight razor near my throat was uncomfortable. After his lecture, he received no tip once I was safely out of the chair. On the TWA flight home to St. Louis, I found the flight attendant of the lightly occupied aircraft failed to waken me for the in-flight meal. When I inquired if there was a chance to get a bite, she let me know directly, 'You missed your chance, soldier boy.' No effort was made to accommodate the Marine who was fighting a war obviously unimportant to her.

Gerard's personal military decorations include Distinguished Flying Cross with Gold Star (2), Bronze Star w/V for Valor, Defense Meritorious Service Medal, Air Medal w/27, Navy and Marine Corps Commendation Medal w/V, Vietnam Campaign Medal with Silver Star (five campaigns) and Republic of Vietnam Bronze Star Cross of Gallantry.

Jug Gerard holding a model of the Bell Helicopter Company's UH-1E (Huey), Brevard NC, 2018

Welcome Home, Brother

David P. Morrow

"Building" Relationships with the South Vietnamese

Construction Battalion (Seabee) insignia

After receiving his draft notice at the end of 1968, North Carolina native David P. Morrow contacted his local Navy Construction Battalion (CB or Seabee) detachment where he was granted a delayed enlistment. "I was one of the luckiest enlistees ever. The postponement afforded me the five months necessary to complete my Associate Degree in Civil Engineering Technology at Southern Polytechnic College in Marietta, Georgia." A week later, Morrow was at Seabee boot camp in Gulfport, Mississippi.

A Team of Thirteen

Assigned to Mobile Construction Battalion (MCB) 5 in Port Hueneme, California, Morrow joined a Seabee Team of 13 men skilled to help Vietnamese rural populations through training, technical assistance and actual construction. Often referred to as the U.S. Navy's own Peace Corps, the Seabee Team consisted of a Civil Engineer Corps officer, eleven Navy enlisted construction specialists, and a hospital corpsman. As an Engineering Aide, Morrow was trained in surveying, drafting and soil analysis. Although each member of the Seabee Team is a specialist, everyone learns the specifics of the other team members' jobs. This cross-rate training results in a very high skill-level of every member, allowing team members to assist each other wherever necessary.

Morrow's Vietnam experience was characterized by the esprit de corps and *Can Do* attitude embraced by a Seabee team, who are together as a unit from team training to their return home from Vietnam. "Belonging to a closely-knit group that went over, worked, and returned together was a huge advantage to my mental well-being."

SERE Training

Seabee team camaraderie, teamwork, and unit cohesion culminated during SERE (Survival Evasion Resistance and Escape) training near San Diego, a specialized course offered to those personnel who might be caught behind enemy lines. The training encompassed those basic skills necessary for survival, search-and-rescue efforts, and evading capture. SERE training was manned by U.S. personnel who had been in-country, and whose job it was to train troops as to what might occur if they were captured. It was highly secret.

"The first night out was on the beach in a huge parachute tent. They gave us fishing lines and hooks, but the water had been fished out and there weren't any fish. On the desert, all the critters were gone, too. We were very hungry. We learned compass and map orientation and marched in the desert's 120-degree heat. Eventually, we were captured and put into a detention camp, a prison modeled after the Vietnamese primitive enclosures with wire fencing and dog houses, where we were interrogated. It was very realistic.

"I was water-boarded. I had heard that if you had long hair, they'd grab it to move you around, so I got a buzz cut. Unfortunately, that indicated that I was a SEAL, or as they called it, a *fish*. I didn't know that. They kept asking me if I was a fish and I said 'No.' So they water boarded me. We had the same reactions that you'd have if you really were captured. However, we learned important lessons. I learned not to get captured! The last morning, everyone assembled in the dirt compound where they took down the Viet Cong flag and raised the American flag while playing the National Anthem. There were a few tears."

After SERE training, the team returned home on leave and then travelled to Point Mugu Navy Air Station. Early one morning in the dark of night, they flew to Vietnam in a four-engine prop plane with several SEAL team members. Morrow was 22.

Training the Locals

In Vietnam, Morrow's Seabee Team 0517 camp was located outside Ben Tre City, Kien Hoa Province, about 60 miles south of Saigon on the other side of the Mekong River. Their mission was to support the government's pacification program to 'win the hearts and minds of the Vietnamese people' through on-the-job training and technical assistance. During their eight-month deployment, Morrow's Seabee Team 0517 completed civic action projects including the construction of badly needed roads, school buildings, warehouses, government offices, a hospital recovery room, and housing units. During their first months there, Seabee Team 0517 was selected as the number 1 Seabee team in Vietnam.

Morrow's job varied from mixing concrete to preparing visual displays of construction progress.

"My job was diverse. I mixed concrete, drove dump trucks, took progress photographs, and organized graphs that depicted the critical path of what needed to be done on each job. Usually we had four-to-five projects going on at once, so I made visual displays for my boss to include in his reports. Each job had its own peculiarities, specific to the Vietnamese culture. For example, in the United States, brick dimensions are relatively similar, each brick is like the next. Not so in Vietnam. There is an art to laying that kind of extruded brick. We purchased the brick, mixed the mortar, then, because their bricks aren't fired like ours, we stuccoed over them to make them waterproof and to strengthen the walls.

"At each of these projects, we had an audience. Vietnamese children were everywhere. They were interested in us because we were Americans and we were generous with things they didn't have." Once, having left his wallet in a shirt pocket on the seat of his truck, Morrow returned to find all his money missing, but his military ID considerately left behind. "We quickly learned to put padlocks on everything, including the fuel tanks on the trucks."

Every project included an audience of curious children.

The *kids* that bothered the Seabee team the most were goats. "The goats were really nasty. They'd jump up in the jeep, walk around the seats, and poop on everything. They just liked to be up high."

Seabee Ingenuity

Seabee Team camps were unlike other military camps in Vietnam. "For several years before our deployment, the area of Kien Hoa Province was so dangerous that the first two Seabee teams were not allowed to leave camp; so, they spent their time building the camp." Morrow's team arrived to find a mechanic's shop, officers' quarters, hot water tanks, a washer and dryer, a bar with air conditioning and an ice machine, flush toilets, showers, and a dining hall that seated 15 people. "We had fresh pineapple and vegetables, and we hired people to do the laundry, so we had clean clothes every day."

The system for building this comparatively luxurious environment was clever. The camp's first team saved money, purchased the equipment (washer, dryer, ice machine, air conditioner) in the U.S. and brought it with them to Vietnam. Successive teams received reduced pay while in training to build up a fund to buy the equipment from the previous team. "When we left, the team that replaced us bought it from us, so we got our money back. The Seabees were ingenious. I don't know what happened to the last team."

CBTeam 0517 was tasked with "winning the hearts and minds" of the South Vietnamese. Viet Cong forces were hesitant to mortar these projects which they knew would be beneficial to them.

Constant Vigilance

"When we first arrived at the camp, we performed alert drills, signaled by a loud telephone bell which rang out in the middle of the night. The objective was to get to our designated bunkers as quickly as we were able, in order to repel the enemy. During the first drill, we showed up in flip flops and underwear, carrying our rifles. We learned the importance of being boots-ready and clothes-ready, and *then* hurrying to the bunker. For many years, every time I heard the old-fashioned phone ring, I'd wake up, totally alert. It took a long time to get over that. It was Pavlovian."

Remaining vigilant was the greatest challenge during Morrow's deployment. "We weren't a high-value target for the Viet Cong because they knew the structures we were building would be useful to them. Nevertheless, we had to worry about who was behind each tree and around every corner. On one occasion, one team member sat down with his back to a tree, facing away from the road. Someone blew up an IED and splattered the tree, but the lucky Seabee was on the other side and survived. And *Charlie* owned the night. The farmers who waved at us during the day as we travelled to the job sites were not our friends at night." [*Charlie* was derived from Viet Cong, or <u>V</u>ictor <u>C</u>harlie.]

Coming Home

Morrow's Seabee Team returned to Port Hueneme in December 1970. While standing in line to get paid, he was told he was eligible for an early out. "I said, 'Thank you very much.' It was just before Christmas and 48 hours later, I was back in North Carolina, stopping only to sleep for eight hours and to purchase snow tires in Knoxville, Tennessee. In January 1971, I returned to Southern Tech."

Returning to college didn't work at first. "I didn't know that I had to decompress from the experience. Sitting in a classroom in January and February, I decided 'I can't do this.' I just needed to spend time outside, able to drive and eat and not worry about having to use my rifle, always remaining vigilant. It took a few months to get back to normal life in the states." The following autumn, Morrow returned to college on the GI Bill and earned a Bachelor of Civil Engineering Technology.

David and his wife Kathy lived in Atlanta and Suwanee for 30 years. David worked for Newbanks & Company, a construction consulting firm for lenders (banks and insurance companies) and Kathy worked at Emory and at the Falcons fitness center. In 2000 they returned to Morrow's hometown of Brevard, NC. Now retired, he was appointed to the County Board of Elections and serves on the Board of Directors of the Veterans History Museum of the Carolinas, once again a member of a Can Do team. "Every time I visit the museum, I learn more about our veterans' history."

David Morrow on a rainy day, inviting passersby to visit the Veterans History Museum (formerly the WNC Military History Museum).

Kathy and David Morrow, 2017

Welcome Home, Brother

Col. Richard G. "Duke" Woodhull, USAF (Ret.)
Flying the Dragon Lady Spy Plane High Over Vietnam

Duke Woodhull, Thailand, 1971

Piloting a spy plane over North Vietnam well above 70,000 feet was a surreal experience for U.S. Air Force Captain Richard Gould "Duke" Woodhull, Jr. Duke Woodhull spent two 60-day tours in Vietnam in 1968 and 1969, piloting high-altitude reconnaissance missions in the Lockheed U-2 aircraft out of Bien Hoa, a Vietnamese installation 40 miles north of Saigon. His was a war of sharp contrasts: the unearthly experience of high-altitude photo reconnaissance versus the reality of daily life on a rough military base in a war zone.

Flying High

Selection to the U-2 program was the realization of a dream for Woodhull. Screening and training for this spy plane, called *Dragon Lady*, were rigorous. Woodhull had 2,500 flying hours when he was selected for the program. The U-2 pilots in Vietnam flew on 7 ½ hour, long-distance missions in a hazardous physiological environment, sealed in a pressurized suit, with the threat of enemy missiles locking on to them.

The U-2 is a unique airplane in that when it taxis out and returns, it is accompanied by a mobile chase car, or *mobile*. Drivers of the mobiles represent a second pair of eyes and ears for the U-2 pilots during takeoffs and landings, making up for the pilot's limited mobility and sight. During day-to-day operations at Bien Hoa, the U-2 pilots alternated between flying the plane and operating the mobile. As one pilot suited up, another pilot drove out to the plane and readied it for flight.

"The U-2 has outrigger wheels which have to be removed before takeoff. The pilot driving the mobile helped the taxiing U-2 avoid ground obstacles, ensured the ejection seat pins were pulled, and performed other pre-launch checks. Once the plane was airborne, the normal climb-out angle was 60 degrees, although it seemed like it was straight up."

The Dragon Lady is difficult to land because it must be fully stalled to land and is susceptible to any type of turbulence. During landing, the chase car, driven by another pilot, assists the U-2 pilot in the air by giving precise advisories about his height above the runway.

U-2 Dragon Lady spy plane original logo: "Toward the Unknown," worn by members of the 329th Strategic Reconnaissance Squadron

"The missions that I flew out of Vietnam were classified and I can't talk about them. It was unreal in the sense that once I'd taken off and was at altitude, I was in another world, completely removed from the experiences of my fellow veterans who flew airplanes low, slow, and under fire. Although, on one mission out of Bien Hoa, I was shot at because it was a mission into an area where we knew there were surface-to-air missiles (SAMs). I saw what looked like a telephone pole coming up at me. It was a SAM, but by the time it approached my altitude it was no longer being directed by its guidance system.

U-2 pilots in Vietnam flew on 7 ½ hour, long-distance missions in a hazardous physiological environment.

"There was always the chance of course that I'd have to bail out and then I'd be in very bad shape. The other aspect of going down was very interesting. We were carrying sensitive classified information on the airplane, defensive systems that had to be protected. We didn't have cyanide needles; but there were switches in the cockpit which would enable us to destroy sensitive electronics in the airplane before we bailed out, assuming we had the time.

"One of our planes did go down. The U-2 is an unforgiving plane and the pilot lost control in the descent, but still over a sensitive area. He had to bail out and the plane crashed. The wreckage contained highly classified equipment, so several days later an Army Special Forces team went in by helicopter, accompanied by the pilot who was familiar with the crash site. Late in the day, they found the wreckage and the classified equipment, but the pilot noticed the Special Forces guys appeared apprehensive. He realized they had to leave the area quickly because there were VC all around. Luckily, they were able to find the equipment, destroy some of it and get the rest out. We did lose some U-2s while I was flying in Vietnam, but not through enemy action. We lost them because the airplane is dangerous to fly and accident prone even though the selection process is vigorous."

War and Violence on the Ground

The air base at Bien Hoa was an old French air force base. Most base residents lived in primitive hooches – wooden structures with screened and jalousied walls designed to capture a breeze in the hot, humid environment. U-2 pilots, due to the physical demands of their assignments and the need to wear pressurized spacesuits, lived in air-conditioned trailers. "You can believe that at the bar all the non-U-2 people ragged us about that. I always felt guilty."

The air base at Bien How was near a river and at night the Viet Cong would approach on the other side, lobbing 120mm mortars at the base. One night the base was heavily attacked, and many aircraft were destroyed. "Just about every night we were treated to this display. The gun ships, the 130s with the cannons shooting out the side, would hose down the area on the other side of the river, or the Army-friendly artillery would tune up and fire multiple rounds into the VC occupied area. We'd be sound asleep, and suddenly we had the sensation of somebody slamming his hand on the side of the trailer. It was only the friendly artillery fire, reminding us of the possibility of a mortar attack that would send us scrambling into the bunker next to the trailer.

"I vividly remember several particularly violent incidents which occurred on base. Besides American planes, the base at Bien Hoa housed Vietnamese A1E fighter planes which carried loads of bombs similar to the B-17s in WWII. Three-ship formations would go out and bomb the Viet Cong. On one occasion three Vietnamese planes took off. Soon two returned and landed, one close behind the other. Both pilots got out of their planes. The first pilot got to the ground and walked over to the other plane. When the second pilot got down to the ground, the first pilot pulled out a pistol and shot him. He killed him on the spot.

I later learned that the Vietnamese flight had been led by the squadron commander.

The pilot who had been shot had been suspected of being insufficiently motivated because during the flight he had reported that his engine was running rough and he wanted to abort the mission. They had to dump the bombs in the river and return to base. Apparently, that was the last straw for the squadron commander. He wasn't going to put up with it anymore. Life on base could be violent, and deadly.

"Another incident, of a similar nature, was equally gripping. There were always a lot of Vietnamese civilians and military on base, constantly driving, walking, and riding bicycles up and down the streets. The Vietnamese army posted sentries to monitor the traffic. One day, they stopped and searched a Vietnamese woman who was pushing a bicycle. In the bicycle basket, a guard found a grenade. He immediately walked her to the side of the road and shot her. I thought to myself, 'Good grief, this is unreal.'"

Woodhull still reflects on the stark dichotomy of living an almost surreal existence during his missions, high above Vietnam, and returning to the realities of war and violence on the ground. "We had a BX (base exchange) -- not much, but it meant a great deal to the young Army soldiers (grunts) who came in out of the field, which might happen to them once during their tour. I could tell that they probably hadn't slept in a long time, had been exposed to things that nobody should be exposed to. I was almost ashamed to approach them, understanding the kind of experience they were having in fighting that war and the kind I was having. I knew the potential for danger to me was great, should I ever have to bail out of my plane. Nevertheless, whenever I'd see a patrol of Army guys, I would be moved by that experience."

Life at Home

"One of the most difficult aspects of a military career is the inevitable family separations. The worst thing about flying the U-2 was the inordinate amount of time away from home which has a negative impact on the family, especially when you have young children. Every veteran who spent time in Vietnam had to cope with this situation. In Bien Hoa, we had no communication. Occasionally my wife would call the squadron and get information indirectly."

Many Vietnam veterans were met with hostility and indifference upon their return home. Woodhull noted that the families of veterans suffered indignities as well. "My wife,

Ann, experienced some really uncomfortable circumstances on the home front. When I was in Bien Hoa, there were times when she received hostile treatment." Later during the war, when Woodhull was in Thailand, Ann joined a *Waiting Wives* group of women whose husbands were overseas, some of whom were POWs and MIA. "Unfortunately, those women were often treated shabbily. It was a far cry from today, when there is a greater appreciation of the sacrifices of the Armed Forces.

"The Vietnam experience was totally compelling for *everyone* in the Armed Forces. You either served, or you knew you'd be serving. There are individuals who never made it there, but it's not because they hadn't signed up and said, 'I'm willing to go.' We were all a brotherhood of arms."

Colonel Duke Woodhull with a retired U-2 at Davis-Monthan AFB, Arizona, 1997

Retirement After 30 Years

Duke Woodhull retired as a Colonel in 1985 after 30 years in the Air Force and immediately went to work for Boeing, assisting them in Brazil on the space station. Today he volunteers with his church, including their Veterans Ministry program, and serves on the Board of Trustees of Blue Ridge Community College. His wife Ann imports high-scale jewelry from Brazil. The couple appreciates living in western North Carolina and being part of a community that recognizes and honors the service of our country's veterans.

Duke Woodhull at Veterans History Museum of the Carolinas, 2018

Duke and Ann Woodhull, 2018

Welcome Home, Brother

RONALD SEVERS
Marine Combat Engineer Trained for Trouble

7th Engineer Support Battalion of the First Marines

"Fasten your seat belts and stay in your seats," said the stewardess on a chartered commercial flight from Okinawa to Da Nang, Vietnam. "We have to make a quick descent." It was 1969 as 18-year-old Ron Severs looked down on the streets of Da Nang, teeming with vehicles, tanks, military personnel and civilians. Severs still remembers that moment. "I thought to myself, 'They're going to shoot at us. This is not a movie; this is the real thing.'"

Severs joined the Marines immediately after graduating from high school in 1968. "I graduated the first week in June, and on June 18th I was at Parris Island. My brother and I left home the same day. He went into the Army and I went into the Marine Corps. I never thought about the impact that had on my poor mother; especially since we all knew where we were going."

The war in Vietnam was escalating in 1968 and Severs' training at Parris Island was cut short by two weeks, as the U.S. military endeavored to get as many boots on the ground as possible. After transport training at Camp Geiger and infantry training at Camp Pendleton, Severs was sent directly to Vietnam.

7th Engineer Support Battalion, "Big Red"

CPL Severs' military operation specialty (MOS) was a truck driver in a combat engineer battalion: the 7th Engineer Support Battalion, First Marine Division, located eight miles southwest of Da Nang. The battalion provided engineering support to the Marine Corps including upgrading and maintaining roads; building lookout towers, helicopter landing pads and gun pads; and sweeping roads for mines. Severs' trucks hauled supplies to different locations, carried gravel, and moved heavy equipment such as bulldozers up and down the roads.

One of the obstacles encountered while hauling supplies was constant theft by the civilian population. "Whenever I drove back from Da Nang with construction materials, children jumped on the truck and started unloading supplies. If we stopped, they took everything, so we just kept moving. We fastened the load down to make it as difficult as possible."

"One day, I took a crew out to re-build a bridge. As I was waiting to load timbers onto my truck, a Vietnamese boy casually walked by me and slit my hip pocket with his razor, hoping my wallet would fall out. He disappeared before I turned around. Praise the Lord, although I was in combat, I never got hit. The closest thing that happened was when that boy tried to cut my pants off."

Security Truck on Mine Sweeping Team

Hauling supplies to work sites occurred only after roads had been cleared by mine-sweeping teams. Severs, in a security truck, and ten-to-twelve men on foot (sweepers), made up the sweep team that surveyed the potentially lethal traffic routes.

Before hauling could occur, minesweepers surveyed the routes. Severs' truck was the first vehicle down the road.

"I drove for the sweep teams the whole time I was in Vietnam. When I was at Camp Pendleton, a gunny sergeant asked me, 'Marine, what's your job?' I told him I was a truck driver. 'Your life expectancy is less than that of a machine gunner. You'll never make it,' he said. A machine gunner's life expectancy in a fire fight was less than six seconds and he was telling me that my odds were worse than that."

Every morning the crew swept a section of road for mines. Severs, in his vehicle, was the last person on the sweep team. Severs' security truck (a five-ton cargo truck with a 50-caliber machine gun) was the first motor vehicle to proceed down the road. The sweepers didn't rely on metal detectors alone because most of the mines were wood. Keen eyesight was critical as the team looked over the shoulder of the road, searching for something unusual that hadn't been there the day before. The enemy harassed the road crews continuously, planting dummy mines as well as live mines, and subjecting the Marines to sniper fire and ambushes. "I went for months doing this every day, knowing that every drive could be my last."

"Civilians would stay behind my truck as we moved down the road. Behind me, people rode their bicycles, trying to get to the next village to sell their products. By the time we finished sweeping the road, there were 50 to 100 people behind us, waiting for us to clear the road. No other military personnel – just civilians.

"We liked to buy ice cream from the kids. But the Viet Cong used that technique to poison us. I learned this when I suffered from severe food poisoning. It was a ploy by the Viet Cong. We got to know them and trust the villagers, then they'd poison the food and vanish. If we asked about someone who had disappeared, the answer was always, 'he beaucoup VC.' We never knew who our enemy was."

Lethal Wooden Pegs in a Box

The VC forces planted improvised land mines with deadly effectiveness. Severs described the simplicity, and sophistication, of some of their land mines. On one occasion, his engineer group was laying a radar cable around Da Nang which would detect the Viet Cong when they approached the area. The combat engineers were harassed continually as they worked on the project.

"Our group was taking a bulldozer out to the construction area and I was driving the security truck carrying a bed full of soldiers. The driver in front of me was pulling a lowbed trailer, carrying the bulldozer. He told me to fall back on the hills because he might not be able to make it to the top. He made it up two hills. He started up the third hill, I fell back, and suddenly, *KABOOM*, the whole back of his truck blew up. Since it was the trailer, the driver wasn't killed. He crawled out, scared to death.

"The VC had been aiming at *my* truck, loaded with infantrymen. They had been watching us and knew how many vehicles were in front of me, so they planted a mine that was designed to withstand the other vehicles until my truck detonated it."

Severs explained how it was done. "The VC put pegs of different lengths in a wooden box. When the first vehicle ran over the box, a peg would break. The second vehicle broke the second peg. Eventually the targeted vehicle would drive over the box, breaking the last peg and detonating the mine. My truck and those of us on it were saved because the enemy hadn't counted the trailer that was pulled behind the vehicle in front of us."

Newspaper clipping of Cpl. R.M. Severs receiving a certificate for Driver of the Month

Combat Engineers Ambushed

Although *Big Red* was a battalion of engineers, the Marines always were prepared to fight as infantry. During the mine sweeps, all eyes constantly searched for snipers. If one was spotted, the engineers quickly became riflemen.

"We were sweeping a road in front of a rice paddy which was bordered on one side by the road and by hedges on the other three sides. As the sweep team passed, a large group of VC, hiding in the hedges, ambushed us. We crossed the road and dove into a ditch, calling back to our hill for reinforcements.

"When reinforcements arrived, we crossed the road and entered the rice paddy. No shots were fired as we moved through the paddy. When we were almost to the enemy, everything blew up. We were caught in the crossfire of machine guns on both sides of the rice paddy. I remember looking up and seeing leaves flying in the air as the machine gun hit the hedges. I thought, 'This is it.' We didn't get shot; Lord only knows why. He took care of us that day."

Combat Engineers on Patrol

Severs remembers holidays in Vietnam with grim humor. "Sometimes we'd have to go out on a Listening Patrol at night. We patrolled outside the perimeter of the hill, listening and watching. If anything was coming, we called back to the hill. During any holiday season – Christmas, New Year's, 4th of July – five or six of us were always put on Listening Patrol. The CO knew we were non-drinking Christians and that we would be sober. Yep, we could count on it, we'd have patrol duty on the holidays."

Severs' worst war experiences were the aggressive assault patrols of ten-to-twelve men assigned to root out the Viet Cong in small villages. "As a good old southern boy, this really tore me up. We had to go into those villages at night, burst into the hooches with dirt floors, and run them out of bed, throwing the beds over, over-turning their tables and trying to find their tunnels. We had intelligence that there were VC in the village, but to me, you just don't treat people this way, even if they're your enemy.

"Unfortunately, in war you see people get killed, and you see death. When I first got there, it upset me; but after I'd been there and seen mutilation and death on a regular basis, it got so it didn't bother me. It's very sad to say that. The villagers were Vietnamese and Viet Cong; we never knew which were our enemy until they tried to kill us."

Extreme Fatigue in Nam and at Home

In 1970, Severs' Charlie Company moved to Bravo Company's hill. He remembers the extremely long days and nights during his final months in Vietnam. "When we got there, we joined their recon group. We were standing watch in the bunkers at night and working our usual jobs during the day. The last three months I was in Vietnam, I had very little sleep -- building during the day and on patrol at night. Sometimes soldiers fell asleep while driving down the road."

When Cpl. Ron Severs returned home, he visited his high school sweetheart, Cathy, leaving her house at midnight. Driving to his grandmother's home, he fell asleep at the wheel, crossing the highway and railroad tracks and waking up as he was flying over the bank. "When I woke up, I thought I was riding in an airplane. Once again, the Lord took care of me. I made it to my grandmother's house, went to bed and slept for eighteen hours. That's how stressful my last few months in Vietnam were."

Severs and Cathy were married one month after his return from war. He noted that the guys in his tent in Vietnam had placed bets on when each of them would receive his *Dear John* letter from the girl back home. Severs was the only soldier whose girl waited for him.

Today, honoring his community's veterans and helping people in need fill Ron Severs' time. After retiring as Polk County's Director of School Transportation, he put his military-acquired truck driving skills to work with Anchor Baptist Church and his own organization, Triumphant Ministry. He provides disaster relief throughout the country, moving church supplies, bibles, pastors and missionaries wherever they're needed. He also volunteers with Asheville's *Hearts with Hands* and performs honor guard ceremonies with the Transylvania County Honor Guard.

Although he doesn't think he suffers from PTSD, Severs admits to periodic sleepless nights fighting the VC, and to suffering from the effects of Agent Orange, especially diabetes, a condition known to have been caused by the toxic defoliant.

"I understand why we were at war – basically to defeat communism. I'm proud I went, and I thought we had a purpose. But it's sad that we never got the South Vietnamese army trained so they could defeat Communism. We pulled out too early – it was a political war."

How did his truck driving in the Marine Corps carry over into civilian relief work? Ron Severs explained: "I remember laying my head down in that rice paddy when the machine gun was shooting over me, and I said, 'Lord, if you get me out of here, I'll serve you the rest of my days.' With a life expectancy of less than six seconds, I came back home uninjured. Today, I trust in the Lord and let Him take care of me."

Top to bottom:

Ron and Cathy at an Honor Guard function.

Ron holding a paper soldier made by a young student for Honor Flight members.

Ron and his grandson Judson Severs take a ride on his tractor.

Welcome Home, Brother

JOHNNY MARTINEZ
Lessons Learned from the Vietnam War

101st Airborne Division
The Screaming Eagles

Johnny Martinez served near the demilitarized zone in Vietnam during 1970 and 1971 with the 101st Airborne Division, known as the *Screaming Eagles*. Like many veterans, Martinez is uncomfortable speaking about his war experiences, except for some of its humorous aspects. And his mission of visiting and listening to the stories of veterans in hospitals and nursing homes offers a message of hope to his Vietnam comrades who suffer from Post-Traumatic Stress Disorder.

After graduating from high school in New York City in 1969, my friends and I planned to take a vacation and tour the country before going to college to play sports. However, when the draft board notified me that my draft number was 12, it was too late to go back to school.

Lesson #1: Stay in school.

Just sign here. I went in for my physical at Fort Hamilton, Brooklyn, NY. They lined all of us up and a soldier started calling off on the ranks: "One, two, three, four, five, *you're* in the Marines; one, two, three, four five, *you're* in the Marines." I was thinking "What the hell is going one?" They explained before each row: "If you volunteer to go into the Regular Army (which is 3 years), you get a choice of occupation which they'll teach you, and you can choose your destination." Since I was facing a 1-in-6 chance of becoming a Marine and going to Vietnam, I said, "Sure, I'll join the Army, study communications, and go to Europe." They said, "Sign Here." After basic, I was shipped to Vietnam.

Lesson #2: Never volunteer!

Martinez at the DMZ, 1971

Martinez's hooch made of sandbags

Ambushed. I'll always remember an experience I had when I was a *cherry boy* (inexperienced soldier.) I was in a convoy north of Hue when we were ambushed. I ran over to our escort tank and lay on the ground beside it thinking, 'This will be the best place to hide.' The tank fired off several rounds of beehive, and the vibration and the noise from the explosion lifted me off the ground. I was covered with dust. What a stupid move! I was pinned down like that for about a half hour.

Lesson #3: Never hide beside a tank!

A trip to Da Nang. After months of heavy fighting around the DMZ, two of us escorted our CO to the airport at Da Nang where he was due to leave for R&R. When we arrived in Da Nang, we went to the PX (base exchange store) to look around while we waited for the CO to process through.

Cpl. Johnny Martinez

While we were in there, a 2nd Lt. in a pressed uniform and spit-polished boots approached us. Spotting our dirty fatigues and dusty boots he said, 'You call yourselves soldiers? You're a disgrace!' He loudly chewed us out, after which we left the exchange.

Our CO spotted us and asked why we weren't in the PX enjoying ourselves. We explained the situation and he said, "Oh really!" We went back in and found the 2nd lieutenant. Our CO locked the lieutenant's heels together and chewed him up and down. He started in the front and finished in the rear. We thought, *That's our boy!"*

Lesson #4: Polished boots do not a soldier make.

During his Vietnam tour, Martinez was contaminated by the highly toxic defoliant, Agent Orange (AO). He bears the consequences to this day and has suffered from soft-tissue sarcoma and pulmonary issues. After extensive chemotherapy, Johnny was recently declared cancer free by his oncologist at the VA. He still suffers from pulmonary issues.

According to the U.S. Department of Veterans Affairs, the VA has recognized that certain cancers and other severe health problems result from exposure to AO and that *some* birth defects among veterans' children are associated with their service in Vietnam.

Johnny believes his three children born after his return suffer from the genetic consequences of AO. The VA is slowly recognizing that certain second-generation conditions are AO-related. Martinez urges concerned citizens to contact their congressional representatives and demand that the investigation into the effects of Agent Orange continues. "Because when all the affected Vietnam vets have died, our children and grandchildren will still be suffering."

Lesson #5: Don't let the VA forget our children.

Another consequence of Martinez's Vietnam tour is severe PTSD. "People don't realize many of the things that really bother soldiers, like sounds or smells. One thing that is still very difficult for me is to hear a baby crying -- from children crying in the villages, I guess."

After many years of coping with PTSD, Martinez found his own personal source of relief: helping other veterans. "At church, the Holy Spirit talked to me. That week's sermon called on parishioners to visit the ill and elderly in nursing homes. It struck me that I could visit veterans at assisted living facilities and hospitals in the county. I thought, 'I'll try it at one place, and I'll visit two veterans and see how it turns out.' Well, as I walked out after the visit, I knew this was my calling. That was 17 years ago and to this very day that's what I'm doing. I've recruited volunteers from the VFW and American Legion, I started a Veterans Ministry at my church. I have some wonderful comrades that joined the ministry, male and female."

Lesson #6: Help yourself through helping others.

Recently during a ceremony in front of his city's courthouse, Johnny Martinez received numerous tributes for his service to veterans in nursing homes and to hospice patients. The honors included two commendations from the City Council and the Mayor's office, including a key to the City of Brevard; acclamations from a U.S. senator and a state representative; and a gift of the North Carolina flag flown over the capitol. Johnny's mission is recognized throughout his community.

Johnny (right) and his friend Spider Trantham are members of the VVA (Vietnam Veterans of America), Chapter 124 in Asheville, NC. The VVA motto is: "Never again will one generation of veterans abandon another."

Johnny Martinez

Johnny Martinez and two of the many veterans whom he visited and who became his close personal friends.

Johnny and a fellow Airorne veteran

Welcome Home, Brother

Maj. Phil Seymour, USMC (Ret.)
The Night of the Spiders

Phil Seymour and a young Vietnamese friend named Cam

Phil Seymour enlisted in the Marines in 1965 and obtained his commission as a 2nd Lt. in 1975. After attending law school and passing the Massachusetts Bar Exam, he returned to active duty as a Judge Advocate, working primarily in trial law. He retired in 1995, after serving at the Pentagon as Head, Law of War Branch, International Law Division, Office of the Judge Advocate General of the Navy. Below, in his own words, is his account of The Night of the Spiders.

Welcome Home, Brother

When two or more veterans get together and discuss their war experiences, they don't talk about how many lives they may have taken in combat, or about their own deeds of valor. Instead, in my experience during three decades of service as both officer and enlisted, vets typically address the friends they served with, the places they were assigned, and the humorous anecdotes they experienced during their tours. This is one such recollection that still manages to bring a smile to my face.

In the late summer of 1967, the war in Vietnam was reaching a crescendo, with close to a half million troops serving in-country and roughly 300 Americans dying in combat each week. By this time, I was well past my half-way mark on a 13-month tour.

Phil Seymour, USMC

I was a sergeant at this time, assigned to the First Platoon in C (Charlie) Company, First Battalion, First Marine Regiment, of the First Marine Division (or simply, C 1/1, for short). By August of '67, I'd been in country for about nine months, had been wounded eight months earlier, and still faced an interminable five months ahead, of what...? That was the big bugaboo, none of us knew what the future entailed; dying, a distinct possibility; wounds, a distinct likelihood; or if lucky, a flight on the freedom bird home. The future was truly uncertain and none of us knew how we'd be going home, or if we'd be going home at all. But, by this time, most of us had accepted the reality of our situation and did not dwell on the possible outcomes. I'd say we'd become fatalistic to our circumstances, but that wouldn't be quite right, as that presumes that events will happen regardless of our actions -- our fate is our fate. But the fact was, the more times one engaged in firefights, walked booby trapped trails, or endured Viet Cong or North Vietnamese ambushes, the likelihood of walking away diminished incrementally.

Operation Pike

The constant rains of the winter monsoon season had given way to the increasingly hot, humid days of summer in our Tactical Area of Responsibility (TAOR) in central I Corps. Of the four Corps regions within South Vietnam, I Corps was the most northern, situated just below the DMZ. 1/1's particular TAOR was located about 20 miles south of the northern port city of Da Nang and comprised roughly thirty square miles around our battalion rear, located near the village of Hoi An. We were back in the battalion rear readying ourselves for an early morning's departure on yet another search-and-destroy operation (designated *Operation Pike*), this one being a sweep of a coastal island about five miles to our south. We drew extra bandoleers of 5.56-millimeter (.223 caliber) ammunition for our M16's, extra M26 fragmentation grenades, and other essential (and heavy) items. Then, after squaring away the rest of our gear, most of us tried to get some sleep, in anticipation of an early departure the following morning.

We were up at 0400. Following a hasty breakfast, we made our way to the Amphibian Tractor (amtrack) park where we climbed atop these lumbering behemoths. These tracks have inside seating, but because of the ever-present danger from anti-tank mines, we considered it at least marginally safer to ride atop, despite the inviting targets we made for Viet Cong snipers.

It was about a 30-minute ride eastward to the coast. Upon rumbling onto the beach, the amtracks each turned hard right and proceeded south in column parallel to the surf. We passed a small fishing village where a dozen or more children ran alongside our vehicles with outstretched hands seeking C-ration candy. We soon arrived at the wide mouth of the Vinh Cua Dai River and plunged into the water for the 500-meter crossing to the island that was our destination.

As we reached the shoreline, the amtracks' treads gained traction on the sand as we headed up about 50 meters into the tree-line. Jerking to a stop, we launched ourselves over the side and took up defensive positions. All was quiet as we scanned the wooded terrain to our front and sides. My platoon of about 30 men was to cross to the western side of this narrow island and we moved off in that direction. Second and 3rd platoons remained on the heavily forested eastern side and prepared to spread out and head south.

The terrain was moderately thick with vegetation, though not as dense as that on the eastern side. Between us and our other two platoons was an open sandy stretch that lacked any semblance of cover and concealment. But as long as we could remain on our western

Marines atop an M-48 tank during a pause in the sweep south. From here, they dismounted and proceeded on foot, following in trace of the tanks who were in the lead.

side of the island, the lack of protective vegetation to our immediate left flank was of limited concern to us. With that, we set out in tactical formation heading south, maintaining our appropriate interval between the Marines to our front, flanks, and rear.

Marines Under Attack

All was blessedly quiet for the first 45 minutes and we moved about a mile-and-a-half south. Then

Marines crossing hazardous terrain

we all heard the staccato bursts of an erupting firefight from the two platoons on the far side of the island. The intensity of the exchange grew quickly until, not unexpectedly, the radio call came for us to cross the open area and add our firepower into the skirmish against a rather large Viet Cong force. I had to admit, the prospect of crossing this vast open stretch was somewhat daunting. Nevertheless, we began the crossing at a slow jog.

Anyone who has ever tried to run in beach sand, especially when weighted down with 50 or so pounds of gear -- helmet, flak jacket, rifle, cartridge belt with spare magazines, two water-filled canteens, grenades, stuffed haversack on our backs, etc. -- knows how difficult this can be. Our slow jog soon deteriorated into a moderately fast shuffle through the sucking sand. Before long, we were all struggling determinedly as we plodded toward the distant tree-line. Not unexpectedly, about half-way across, the left flank of the Viet Cong force shifted much of its base of fire toward us. Lacking any protective cover, we had no option but to continue our arduous trek toward the still distant tree-line.

As we approached the tree-line and some measure of protection, I felt (and heard) an impact on my left hip and my immediate thought was, "I've been hit." I began an assessment of my own situation and found no apparent wound around my hip area. We continued the final yards and fell in behind the cover of a thick stand of pine trees.

Miraculously, none of the others who made the crossing with me were hit as well. With the addition of our firepower to that of the other two platoons, the Viet Cong unit soon began to disengage from the firefight. We could not tell just how far this force had pulled back, or whether they had moved at all. But of more immediate concern was attending to the few casualties from this skirmish. Our company commander called in a medivac helicopter for the casualties. We had one dead, the CO's radioman, and several wounded; bad, but certainly not as bad as it could have been, given the size of the Viet Cong force and the volume of fire they put out. It wasn't until after things quieted that I sought a swig of water from my canteen. It was then that I discovered that the impact I had felt earlier was that of a Vietcong round passing through my canteen that I carried on my left hip, a far more acceptable target than my hip itself!

Digging In for the Night

By the time the medivac helicopter arrived, it was nearing sunset and time to establish a secure "360 perimeter" for the night. This would be a moonless night and visibility would be next to zero. We waited until darkness had set in before assigning two-man positions and having everyone dig-in for the night. This was to help ensure that the Viet Cong would not know where our positions were with any degree of certainty. The word was passed around for everyone to stay in his respective position, no matter what, and that anyone out of his hole would likely be Viet Cong and shot.

We each dug shallow fighting holes. For mine, I added a shelf of sorts for my rifle, extra magazines, and grenades, and stuck my bayonet in alongside the other articles, hoping beyond hope that I'd not have to use it. The nighttime temperature was probably only in the 70's, but the contrast with the intense heat of the day made it seem quite cold. To combat the night's chill, I pulled my mosquito netting over me with the hope of retaining some degree of body heat. Preparations complete, I settled in for what I knew was to be a long and sleepless night.

Uninvited "Guests"

Soon I felt light, almost tickling movement on both of my legs. With the intense heat of the day, we wore our jungle utility trousers un-bloused; i.e., loose trouser cuffs around our jungle boots, in order to facilitate better air circulation. Likewise, we wore our jungle utility jackets (shirts actually) loose to allow for air circulation as well. Additionally, none of us wore underwear, as we were neither issued any, nor could we keep underwear from simply rotting and tearing in the stultifying humidity. Thus, it was not at all surprising that crawling things, usually just blood-sucking land leaches, would find their way up and around our bodies at night while in the field (this being about 99 percent of the time).

In this case, however, the movement I was feeling was not that of the slow crawling leaches. I took my small flashlight with the red lens and played it's beam down onto and then under the mosquito netting covering my legs. What I saw (and felt) were a dozen or more large, medium brown, hairy, long legged spiders moving with determination up my legs, both inside and out of my utility trousers. I could also see more beginning the climb up my trouser legs as well. I knew that before long they would also be on and under my utility jacket. Now these weren't your ordinary dime-size spiders. These were spiders whose eight long, hairy legs would easily overlap a C-ration can. In other words, their leg span was on the order of four or five inches! They were not as thick-bodied or thick-legged as tarantulas, but they were nonetheless huge. I had seen innumerable varieties of vermin over the past nine months, though I had never encountered arachnids such as these before.

What to do? Were they poisonous or were they harmless? I hadn't a clue. What I did know was that picking up and moving to a different location was not an option. Could I kill them? Possibly. But, if they were poisonous, without being stung? Probably not. The only viable option was to grin and bear it. There was nothing to do but to let them creep and crawl to their tiny hearts' content. And that's exactly what they did.

The night's entertainment seemed to stretch on interminably. They crawled and explored just about everywhere possible. My private areas were not off limits, nor were my armpits, face, or head. Not knowing whether they were venomous limited my ability (and willingness) to brush them off my face and other important body parts. If there was any saving grace, however, it was that I didn't struggle to stay awake, even in the wee hours. And they continued to crawl.

At long last, the gradual brightening toward the eastern edge of the tree line suggested dawn was approaching at long last. Though I was largely unaware of it, as if on cue, my *friends* slowly began making their way back from whence they had come. One by one, their numbers diminished. Finally, with enough faint light to assess my surroundings, I was able to examine my hole and determine what this whole episode had been about. Checking down where my feet had been, I saw the source of the night's visitors. Apparently, when digging my fighting hole in the darkness the night before, I had inadvertently dug into a large underground spiders' nest. In retrospect, given the intense heat of the day, I suspected that this variety of spider had become nocturnal wanderers, seeking what little food and moisture they might find in the cooler temperatures of night.

I'd had little choice but to refrain from killing these creatures and they, in turn, had elected to refrain from biting or stinging me. All things being relative, having these critters wander over my body all night had not been among my more immediate concerns. The prospect of being bitten or stung was not as onerous as the bite or sting of a Viet Cong bullet. I judged that I had spent far worse nights in the field and would yet again!

Upon rising and heating our B-1 cans of a C-ration breakfast, I could not help but share the previous night's entertainment with the half dozen Marines sitting in my small grouping. With humor being in relatively short supply, this rather trivial event did manage to bring a smile (and a couple of choice retorts) to the otherwise somber faces around our morning's C-ration coffee klatch.

Above: Lynne and Phil Seymour

Left: Phil holding the canteen which took a bullet for him during the day of the night of the spiders.

REAR ADMIRAL GRADY L. JACKSON, USN (RET.)

Fighting the War from the Air

In boxing, the Sunday Punch is the most powerful and effective punch of a boxer. In the armed forces, it is anything capable of inflicting a powerful blow on a hostile or opposing force.

In April 1972, Lt. Cdr. Grady L. Jackson was the senior Bombardier/Navigator (B/N) assigned to VA-75 *Sunday Punchers*, home ported at Naval Air Station Oceana in Virginia Beach, Virginia. As a Navy medium attack squadron, VA-75 flew the A6A Intruder all-weather night attack aircraft, assigned to AirWing 3, and deployed aboard USS *Saratoga* (CV-60). The A6A was crewed by a pilot and a B/N sitting beside the pilot in the cockpit; they were separated by a low instrument panel with various radio and other controls, accessible by both. The control stick for the aircraft was in front of the pilot, between his legs and the radar scope was in front of the B/N, between his legs. The A6A was capable of carrying various large ordnance loads, and could fly for long distances, and also had the capability for air-to-air refueling.

The USS *Saratoga* was home ported at Naval Station Mayport, Florida; however, the many AirWing aircraft were stationed at various Naval Air Stations situated along the East Coast. The year prior, the USS *Saratoga* and AirWing 3 team had completed a seven-month deployment to the Atlantic Ocean and Mediterranean Sea. Many of the *Saratoga*/AirWing wives, including Grady's wife Linda, joined their husbands for several days in Athens, Greece. Everyone was looking forward to another enjoyable deployment.

However, their lives were turned upside down when they received an unexpected phone call one Saturday morning from the squadron duty officer who told them to pack their cruise boxes and bring them to the squadron hangar on Sunday. They were told by the duty officer that they were now scheduled to fly their A6A/KA-6D/A6B aircraft on Tuesday and land aboard USS *Saratoga* off the coast of Florida. Although they were not told where the ship and AirWing were headed, everyone correctly surmised that they would soon be flying day/night strike missions over North and South Vietnam.

It was difficult for Grady to leave behind his wife Linda (married almost eleven years), and their eight-year-old son Daniel and five-year-old daughter Christina, not knowing when he would return. Grady experienced mixed feelings. "On a professional level I was truly excited that I finally was going to be able to utilize my thirteen years of flight training and fly real combat missions in the A6A/A6B."

As an all-weather day/night attack aircraft, the Intruder was capable of being configured with extremely large loads of various kinds of ordnance, which made it very effective in leading daytime coordinated AirWing strikes. However, the mission in which the aircraft and aircrew excelled above all other AirWing aircraft was the single-aircraft low-altitude (below 500 feet) night strike.

After a month-long transit from Mayport, Florida they arrived at Subic Bay, Philippines to resupply the ship and AirWing. Each day during the long transit, the aircrew received detailed briefs by squadron experts to help prepare them for combat operations over North Vietnam and on how to survive.

Combat Missions in the North

After a port call in Subic Bay, which included more survival training, they arrived in the Tonkin Gulf in June 1972. The first combat missions were over South Vietnam, in support of U.S. personnel on the ground, and controlled by airborne Air Force Forward Air Controllers or FACs. During these missions, the greatest threat to the aircraft was to make sure that they didn't fly under a B-52 strike, which dropped tons of bombs on one run from a very high altitude.

"But to be honest, no amount of ready-room intelligence briefings could adequately prepare you for the high warble audio sound of *deedle-deedle-deedle* in your helmet of a surface-to-air missile tracking your aircraft in the daytime. Thankfully, the AirWing tactical aircraft were more maneuverable than the missile, which looked like a flying telephone pole; nevertheless, AirWing aircraft were hit by the surface-to-air-missiles when the aircraft did not see it and therefore didn't maneuver.

A-6 Intruders flying over Vietnam

At night, enemy radar could not track or guide on our aircraft at 500 feet and below; however, that did not stop their Anti-Aircraft Artillery (AAA) barrage fire (which we could see because of the red tracers, interspersed in the AAA). At night the F-4 Phantom fighters, who flew Barrier Combat Air Patrol off the coast of North Vietnam, would tell us after our mission at the AirWing debrief that they could follow our flight path by the AAA red tracer fire along our route as we headed to our target inland."

Grady Jackson with an A-6 Intruder. The A6A could carry large ordnance loads, fly long distances, and had the capability for air-to-air refueling.

In the daytime, the AirWing would normally fly three major Alpha strikes, which involved just about every type of AirWing aircraft in a coordinated strike against a major target over North Vietnam. As the senior B/N, Grady flew mostly night strikes with the Commanding Officer Charlie Earnest, a true combat leader who had prior Vietnam combat experience in the A4 aircraft. Grady also flew with the AirWing Commander Deke Bardone on many daytime Alpha strikes. Grady's professional opinion is that both Skipper Earnest and CAG Bardone were two of the Navy's best and most capable combat leaders.

One of Grady's favorite stories from Vietnam is the incredible rescue of Lt. Jim Lloyd on the night of 6 & 7 August, 1972. Lt. Lloyd was flying an armed recon flight over North Vietnam, about 150 miles north of the DMZ. Lloyd was flying in an A7A single-seat aircraft, as the wingman of a flight of two A7 aircraft. As darkness set in, his aircraft was hit by a surface-to-air missile, which required immediate ejection from his aircraft 21 miles inland.

The Rescue of Lt. Jim Lloyd

"CDR Charlie Earnest, CO of the Sunday Punchers, was my pilot and we took over as Search and Rescue (SAR) On Scene Commander (OSC) about an hour after Jim was shot down. That meant the decision of whether to try to rescue Lt. Lloyd was in our hands. By the time we arrived feet-dry over the beach, after taking on 6-8,000 pounds of gas, it was totally dark. However, we had received a good debrief over the radio from the first OSC on where Jim was located.

"Flying at 500-1000 feet, we immediately established radio contact with Jim by taking up a heading of 070 degrees and seven miles from an easily identified bend in a river, which I could see visually and on my radar.

"Too many people were around Jim, and they were calling his name – *Jeem, Jeem* -- so he asked us to move away from his position. We went back inland near the river still flying at low level, in order to coordinate the rescue effort and to get away from the increasing anti-aircraft artillery in the area.

"Later we learned that Jim had lost his hand-held radio out of his G-suit, after crawling about 100 yards from his initial hiding place. No radio, no rescue! So, he crawled back on his hands and knees and found his radio.

"As Jim was trying to get farther away from the fiery wreckage and from the people who were looking for him, he heard footsteps along the path, which was around a rice paddy. It was not very wide, so he lay face-down in the muddy paddy and played dead. Soon the footsteps stopped, and he felt someone poking him in the back with what felt like a gun. He heard two men speaking excitedly in Vietnamese, and then footsteps leaving. Sensing that this was his best chance of escape, he slowly turned over and found that both had gone for help. He used this opportunity to jump up and run the opposite direction along the dirt path of the rice paddy, with bullets flying all around him.

"Almost 3½ hours had passed since Jim's ejection from his burning aircraft and time was quickly running out for his rescue. The H-3 'Big Mother helicopter with its two pilots, hoist operator, and 60cal door gunner had been delayed due to refueling problems.

"This night rescue, over enemy territory, was in the days before rescue helicopters were equipped with Terrain Following Radars, night vision goggles and GPS. All the Big Mother aircrew possessed to fly just over treetops at night was a radar altimeter and a lot of guts! Finally, they were refueled and had two A7's as escorts from the carrier USS *Midway* because the *Saratoga* had ceased flight operations.

"As On Scene Commander, it was our responsibility to make the decision whether or not to call in our AirWing helicopter, now escorted by USS *Midway* A7's. Immediately the Skipper and I flew back to where we thought Jim was located; however, we couldn't establish radio contact. No radio contact meant no rescue! I quickly radioed the helo/A-7 escort rescue team and told them to hold their position, which was now over enemy territory. I thought to myself, 'Way to go, Grady. You are now risking the lives of the helicopter crew, and the two A7's escort crews and you don't have radio contact with Jim Lloyd!'

"In desperation, I cried out a very short prayer, 'God, help!' Immediately, the thought came to me to fly back to the bend in the river and take up the exact 070 degrees heading for seven miles and try again. As soon as we did, I established radio contact with Jim. By this time, his radio batteries were getting very weak, which meant we had to be almost on top of him to receive his radio transmissions.

"With positive radio contact we could now redirect the H-3 helicopter and escorting A7's. To aid them, the Skipper turned on our outside aircraft lights so the rescue team could now vector on us. However, this also gave the AAA sites a target to shoot at, but a target much more maneuverable than the large and slow Big Mother helicopter.

"Because of Jim's weak radio, I had to relay all the radio transmissions between Jim and the rescue helicopter, since they couldn't hear or talk directly to each other. Also, all radio transmissions were now being conducted on the Universal Guard Channel, which meant the whole world was hearing in real time the Jim Lloyd rescue operation.

"Our USS *Saratoga* H-3 helicopter was now flying further into North Vietnam than any Navy helicopter during the Vietnam War. In fact, we learned years later that the helicopter crew was very uneasy about the terrain ahead of them, so they made the decision to turn on their landing lights, which illuminated a very large piece of real estate. As soon as they turned on their landing lights, they realized that they were heading into a small mountain ridge and some trees, and they had to do a quick pull-up to miss them.

"In doing so, their landing lights had given the H-3 pilots temporary night blindness. They didn't see Jim and flew right over him. In our A6, with a bird's eye position above the rescue scene, I could see Jim Lloyd in a rice paddy frantically waving his arms. Jim told us later that all around him there were North Vietnamese troops closing in to capture him. Observing the scene from our position above, I screamed in the radio for Big Mother to make a 180-degree turn.

"As they were making the turn back to Jim, the Skipper and I saw a big burst of fire from a 57mm gun, which looked like it could not miss the helicopter. But it did! The helo, which now had Jim in sight, lowered its rescue cable with the jungle penetrator hooked to the end. When Jim saw the penetrator on the ground, he quickly attached it to his torso harness. Because his back was to the helicopter, he didn't notice that it was hovering over the rice paddy in order to avoid anti-aircraft fire and getting stuck in the mud.

"The hoist operator yelled for Jim to get in the open door. Finally, as Jim jumped as high as he could, the door gunner grabbed him by his flight suit and threw him into the cabin with an adrenaline-fueled heave. They turned off their lights and, despite several bullet holes which could have been critical, they made it back to the ship.

"After depositing eight rock eye cluster weapons on that AAA site and refueling from a KA-6D tanker from our squadron, the Skipper and I made it back to the *Saratoga*. We logged 3.8 hours of flight time that night, most of it over North Vietnam, by far the longest flight we had ever experienced over enemy territory!

"In the end, no one had a scratch on them, including Jim Lloyd. This successful Navy rescue was one of the deepest in enemy territory during the war. Many people risked their lives to rescue Lt. Jim Lloyd: two of our A-7 guys, the Skipper and I, Midway's A-7's, and the Big Mother's helo crew of four. That night we showed the world that if you go down, the United States Navy will do everything they can to keep you from being a POW or killed."

Seven Seconds to Life and Death

At 0200 on November 28, 1972, after 150 strikes, LCDR Jackson and Skipper Earnest were called to launch against a convoy of trucks. That night the Airwing was in 'stand down' and not supposed to be flying. A maintenance crew had been working on a radar repeater scope, located on the flight instrument panel in front of the pilot's flight control stick. The maintenance crew left to eat their midnight meal, and the bolts had not yet been installed. Not knowing this, the aircraft was assigned for this add-on mission.

"As soon as the catapult fired, the scope, which was not bolted down, slid out of the brackets and lodged itself against the pilot's control stick. We both saw it happen; however, for the first few seconds there was nothing we could do, as the G-forces had us pinned against our seats.

"At that moment a voice told me 'If the Skipper gets the nose of the aircraft over (we were now climbing to the stars because the stick was full aft), stay with it. But if the aircraft rolls left or right, get out!' Immediately the aircraft made a roll to the right and I raised both hands over my head and grabbed and pulled the face curtain, which initiated my ejection from the aircraft.

I was sitting on a 200-pound rocket sled that thrust me and my seat through the plexiglass canopy at approximately 25 G-forces. Because of the G-forces, I blacked out. My parachute automatically deployed, slowing my descent into the water." The time from catapult launch to water impact was just seven seconds.

The first Jackson remembered after ejecting was being in the water, tangled in his parachute. He ripped off his oxygen mask to breathe. After 35 minutes in the water, he was picked up by the H-3 rescue helicopter. Although Jackson was slightly injured, they spent another 30 minutes airborne, searching for Skipper Earnest. "But I knew he had not ejected. He was too preoccupied with trying to save the aircraft. Skipper Charles M. Earnest was a brilliant Naval Officer, an incredible leader and a highly respected combat air warfare tactician. I not only lost my Commanding Officer, but my pilot and a real friend."

During the Vietnam War, Jackson received three Silver Stars along with eight Distinguished Flying Crosses and other combat awards.

A Changed Life

Admiral Grady L. Jackson

"I remember, just like it was last night, floating in the Tonkin Gulf, afraid I was going to drown, crying out: 'God, get me out of this, but I am not ready to change my life.' I think God looked down at me and said, 'Look son, I know that you are going to change your life!' God answered my very honest prayer and on the morning of November 28, 1972, my life was given back to me and it has never been the same since."

Jackson, who retired as a Rear Admiral in 1991, is glad to see Vietnam veterans honored in the *Transylvania Times*. "We forget that our military servicemen and women and their families sacrifice many things in service to our country. The Vietnam War had a very negative connotation for many people. But that doesn't negate what our veterans did -- because that's what it was their duty to do. So many lives were lost for others' freedom, so many gave so much and then, our political leaders gave up and abandoned the freedom cause. Don't go to war if you're not going to finish it."

Intruders pencil drawing made for Grady by a friend.

Today Grady and Linda Jackson live in BrightView, a Senior Living retirement complex in Annapolis, Maryland, near their daughter and family. They encourage and support a medical missions ministry *(Vets With a Mission)* that takes doctors, nurses and other personnel back to Vietnam to assist the people in the many medical needs there. Grady was a past national President of Officers Christian Fellowship and now serves as a President Emeritus, enjoying opportunities to influence and interface with Naval Academy Midshipmen and personnel.

Note:
Vets With a Mission was founded in 1989 and for more than 20 years has implemented various humanitarian programs and projects in the country formerly known as the Republic of South Vietnam. Over 1,600 volunteers, mostly Vietnam vets, have participated on medical teams, ministry teams, disaster relief, or project teams. http://www.vetswithamission.org/

Dr. Steven Salsburg
On Board as a U.S. Naval Flight Surgeon

Helicopter Squadron HML-167 patch

Dr. Steven "Steve" Salsburg was in his last year of internship at Jackson Memorial Hospital during the Vietnam War's Tet Offensive. The escalation of U.S. involvement in Vietnam required more doctors and corpsmen, and Salsburg realized that he probably would be drafted. "On my way home from my internship, I stopped in at the Navy Department in Washington, D.C. Of the options available, I chose U.S. Naval Flight Surgeon."

After six months of flight training, Salsburg was assigned to the Marines at Camp Pendleton for two weeks of basic training for doctors and corpsmen, followed by training with a tanker squadron, practicing mid-air refueling.

"In May 1970, I flew to Vietnam. We got into Da Nang at about 3 a.m. and I jumped into a cot in the officers' barracks. We were a half mile from Liberty Hill where they had an artillery unit. At about 4 a.m. the artillery unit started firing salvos by the huge howitzers, which were so loud that it knocked me out of bed. Some guys on their second tour were standing around smoking, and they watched me fall and flop around for a while. They thought it was pretty funny."

Salsburg (whose Vietnam nickname became *The Quack*) moved across the river to the Marine Air Facility at Marble Mountain, one of five mountains located south of Da Nang that stretched from the coast inland. He was assigned to Marine Air Group (MAG) 16, helicopter squadron HML-167. After several weeks associating with helicopter pilots and crews, Salzburg knew he wanted to fly the choppers. Learning that Salsburg had never flown a chopper, the commanding officer eventually agreed to let him fly with a test pilot on injured birds after they had been through maintenance.

The pilots taught the eager physician how to fly the helos. "After two or three weeks, one of the test pilots told the CO that I could fly well enough to get us out of trouble if a pilot was injured. From then on, I was in. They wouldn't let me fly gunships, I think they were afraid it was a violation of the Geneva Convention, so they put me on the helicopter taxi squad, flying Marines from landing zones to airfields, bases and hospitals.

Medical Treatment Near Da Nang

According to the Navy Medicine Operational Training Center, the naval flight surgeon practices preventive medicine first and foremost.

> "He or she is the interface between the practice of medicine, the science of safety, and the profession of aviation. Through successful aviation medicine programs, the flight surgeon promotes aviation safety, decreasing the potential for aircraft accidents. This is accomplished by a dedicated search for those problems -- physical, mental, environmental, and man-made, which compromise safety in the air and in the workplace."

The physical injuries Salsburg treated were primarily accidents which occurred around machinery, although there were occasional injuries to the Vietnamese locals. "The biggest wound I treated was a child injured by shrapnel. I had the mother bring him back every day for a shot of penicillin. I wasn't comfortable sending him home with pills since the VC, if they found out, would have killed him and kept the pills."

But there were also psychological injuries that needed attention.

A Marine Pilot's PTSD

"One night, one of the guys in my squadron came up to me crying. He'd been flying a general in an attack mission on a village that was supposed to be empty. The Viet Cong had been using it as a supply base and using the civilians as cover. The South Vietnamese Army was supposed to have removed all the civilians so we could destroy the village. The general called in an airstrike and the Phantoms came in, dropping napalm. Just as one plane dropped its load, a small boy ran out of a thatched roof house -- and the napalm just rolled him up.

"The Marine, who had young children of his own, witnessed this and was a mess. When I think of what I had to do next, I wonder how I became so objectively callous about it. After sitting and listening to him and telling him the usual, 'it's not your fault, you'll be ok, your kids are fine,' I went back to my hooch, called the operations officer who scheduled pilots, and told him to take this Marine off the gun ships. I didn't want him to be in a position where he might hesitate, and Marines could be hurt. In retrospect, I think that's the most callous thing I've ever done. About a week later, I passed him as he was yelling 'Why am I on these taxis?' And I said, 'You're ready,' and I put him back on the gun ships."

Visiting a Leper Colony

During his Vietnam tour, Salsburg was assigned to a Medical Civilian Action Program (MEDCAP) in which Americans set up clinics to examine the civilian population. Salsburg's CO received notification that they would visit a leper colony outside Da Nang. Salsburg and other members of the MEDCAP were helicoptered in and out of the colony.

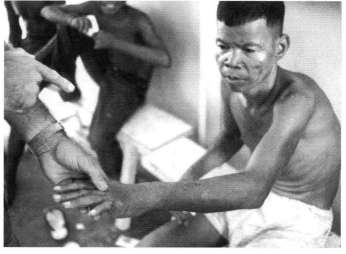

A patient with Hansen's disease. Photo by Dr. Steven Salsburg

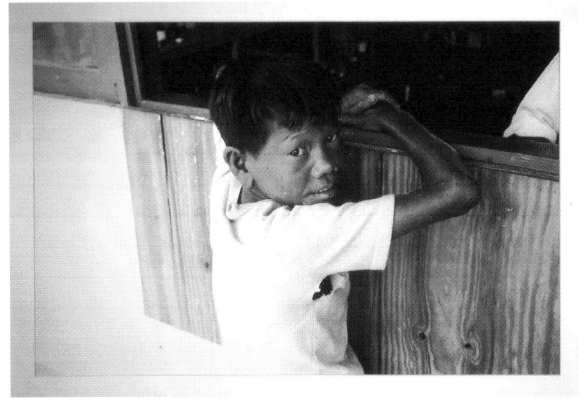

Families accompanied patients with Hansen's disease (leprosy) and stayed until their family member was discharged. Photo by Dr. Steven Salsburg.

"The leper colony, run by Swiss nuns, was in the jungle, a little northwest of Da Nang. Families accompanied the patients and stayed there until the patients were discharged. The lepers were treated with rifampicin. Like TB, Hansen's disease takes a long time and a lot of medication to control.

"A few weeks after we had MEDCAP, the Viet Cong mortared the place and killed some people. I don't know how many of those kids and people were injured in the attack. I think the VC specifically targeted the colony because the nuns had allowed us to visit."

Salsburg's Undetected PTSD

Salsburg described his own long-undetected experience with PTSD. "One morning, we flew into a very small landing zone in *Indian Country*-- dense jungle near Laos – to pick up a Marine colonel and his staff and take them to another base. After we landed, the Marine Executive Officer spoke with the helicopter pilot, who then told me, 'You've got to get out.' I said, 'What do you mean, I have to get out?' Apparently, the Marine colonel had his wings and wanted to fly back in my chair as a co-pilot so he could get his monthly flight pay, about $200. I said 'OK, I'll get in the back.' The pilot said, 'No, he's got too much staff with him, it'll be too heavy. You have to stay here until I come back to get you.' I said, 'Stay where?' There was nothing but jungle and nobody else around. The pilot replied, 'hunker down and I'll come back as soon as I can.' I stepped out onto the foot plate, and that's the last thing I remember for two days."

Salsburg says his mind shut down due to the stress of the situation. He knows that he hid behind the bushes, pulled out his .45 and prepared to fight. But he doesn't remember any of it. "I thought I was fine. But a year later I started drinking, depressed and suicidal. I didn't attribute it to Vietnam, because I didn't have any flashbacks, dreams or memories of the event. My memory was shot. So, I did have the symptoms of PTSD, even though I didn't have the memory of it.

"Back home, I was in the second year of my residency, when one night I was extremely depressed and thinking of suicide. It scared me, so I went to the student psychiatric clinic and started getting psychological help. For the next 30 years, I saw psychiatrists, psychologists and therapists on and off. Not one of them ever asked me if I had served in the military or had been under fire!"

Agent Orange and Some PTSD Relief

Salsburg was one of more than two million American service men and women who were exposed to the toxic defoliant, Agent Orange. At age 55, the results of his exposure were so severe that he had to retire from his career as an ophthalmologist. He decided that while still able, he would train to practice psychiatry. While in his psychiatric residency, he served at the VA as part of his training.

"I was assigned to interview Vietnam veterans who had PTSD. As I sat and listened to them telling me that 'I did this, and I felt like this,' I realized I'd done and felt the same things. After several interviews, I approached the head of the PTSD unit, and after 20 minutes of talking to me he said, 'Yeah, you've got it.'

"Nobody ever put it together because I'd never had any flashbacks or dreams. I'd forgotten them all. I eventually spent time at the Batavia Veterans Hospital in the PTSD unit. And the best thing that happened to me is that I realized I wasn't alone, nor was I as bad off as some others. I'm doing all right now. I have trouble sleeping, but that's about it."

Due to his exposure to Agent Orange, Salsburg has developed two types of cancer, a brain tumor, diabetes, and peripheral neuropathy. "We couldn't see Charlie under the triple canopy jungles, so an herbicide mixture containing the highly toxic chemical dioxin was sprayed at concentrations six-to-ten times higher than recommended.

Agent Orange fell upon forests, crops, civilians and soldiers.

My endocrine system shut down. Diabetes, high blood pressure, coronary heart disease, and neuropathy are now acknowledged by the VA as resulting from Agent Orange exposure. The other symptoms, although suffered by many other veterans, have not yet reached the 'statistical level of significance' qualifying for government benefits. We were hammered with that stuff."

Japan and Flight Training on F-4 Phantoms

In the autumn of 1970, the Marines began pulling out of Vietnam. Steve Salsburg was sent to Iwakuni, Japan where he spent time as a flight surgeon for the Phantom 4 fighter squadron. "I had 40 hours of backseat time in the F4. It was probably like what a video game is for the kids now. We would go on maneuvers, flying combat situations against each other. The Marines that went through top gun at Miramar put on a kind of *Reader's Digest* version of *How to Fight a Mig*. I sat in on some of those programs."

Dr. Steven Salsburg, 2018

The Moment the Street Stopped

Salsburg related his worst military experience. It occurred *before* he went to Vietnam. "A colonel from our base went to Vietnam as a new commander of an A4 attack fighter squadron and was killed. I was asked to be part of a CACO call (casualty assistance condolence call) to inform the wife that her husband was killed. It was a beautiful day in Southern California, a suburban place, sun shining, kids playing, birds singing, wives walking up and down. We pulled up in front of the house and got out in our uniforms. And the street stopped. The kids stopped, the wives came to their doors, it seemed as if the birds stopped singing. That was the worst moment for me. The worst."

Welcome Home, Brother

DAVID SMALE
Scramble the Seawolves

HA(L)-3, Helicopter Attack Squadron (Light) 3, nicknamed the Seawolves

On October 31, 1966, two Navy river patrol boats (PBRs) encountered a superior fleet of sampans and junks intent on transferring a battalion-sized Viet Cong unit from one riverbank to the other. The patrol boats came under intense fire from both sides of the bank, a call for air support went out and HC-1 Detachment (Det) 25 under the command of the Army arrived fifteen minutes later. While the PBRs acted as decoys to pinpoint enemy positions, Det 25 opened fire and forced a retreat through rice paddies.

HA(L)-3, nicknamed *"Seawolves,"* evolved from an Army-directed to a dedicated naval squadron of helicopter gunships in Vietnam. Due to the Brown Water (river) Navy's early successes in the Mekong River Delta, it was decided that the U.S. Navy needed to provide air support rather than the Army.

The Seawolves soon supported Naval Special Warfare operations and the Mobile Riverine Forces in Vietnam. Helicopter Attack Squadron (Light) 3 or HA(L)3, was officially commissioned in South Vietnam on April 1, 1967. Missions included search and destroy, reconnaissance, medevac, SEAL team insertion and extraction. Decommissioned on March 16, 1972, the Seawolves flew more than 120,000 combat missions during the

Vietnam War. It was the only Navy squadron commissioned and decommissioned during the Vietnam War.

The following is the account of a Navy Seawolf, David Smale, who served two tours of duty in Vietnam from 1969 to 1971.

A Seawolf's Story

Our detachment was made up of two UH-1B (Huey) helicopters -- beaten up, underpowered Army castoffs, some of which had 6,000 hours on them. We were always overloaded to the capacity of the helicopter and often had to throw out ammo and drop the rocket pods to get lift. It was not uncommon to run beside the bird until it got some lift, then jump inside.

The Seawolf mission was to support the Brown Water (river) Navy, PBRs and SEAL teams, often in remote locations where there were no roads. Because of our experience and reputation, we often helped others in need: Army, Marines and Special Forces, including inserts and extractions. Over the course of six years the squadron performed more than 1,500 medevacs.

From Ski Slopes to Sea Wolf

In 1968, I had no desire to go to Vietnam, and if I hadn't been a ski bum, I might not have. But I took off a semester from school to go skiing. After several weeks, I called home and was notified that my draft notice had arrived. I was able to join the Navy and after several training schools, I landed in aviation ordnance with orders to HA(L)-3, which none of us had heard of. I arrived in Vietnam on June 6, 1969 and was assigned to an aviation ordnance maintenance shop.

In HA(L)-3, the door gunners and pilots were all volunteers. When the commanding officer asked for volunteers for door gunners, I raised my hand. I was assigned to Detachment (Det) 7. I had never fired an M-60 in my life and my only helicopter experience had been in a small helicopter over Niagara Falls as a teenager. While flying from the maintenance facility out to Det 7, the new petty officer in charge looked at me thinking, "What in the world are they sending out to me?" I was as green as grass, but within three weeks I had figured it out. Eventually I became very good at what I did.

Fortunately, the Seawolf squadron had Navy aviators who were instrument-trained and had learned their craft in fixed wing aircraft which offered longer, more extensive and broader training. These pilots often referred to us door gunners as their secret weapons, because with a full free-hand M-60, we could get close to the friendly forces and still have complete control over the weapon and where the bullets would go.

Medevacs and Mercenaries

Seawolves performed medical evacuations only when there was no chance of anyone else coming soon or when somebody's life was at stake. My first experience occurred when a soldier's leg had been blown off by a booby trap. It was a grim operation and an eye-opener to me about the day-to-day job of the Army's dust-off crews. (Dust-off crews consisted of two pilots, a medic and a crew chief.)

Seawolf David Smale during Det 1; post-mission replenishment.

My first exposure to the mountain mercenaries known as the Montagnards was at Moc Hoa, a remote area near the Cambodian border where a Green Beret unit was stationed. On our arrival, we noticed that the Montagnards wore necklaces made from human ears. We thought, "We're not in Kansas anymore."

Flying with Living Legends

In 1970, I extended for another six months in Vietnam. When asked whether I would like to transfer to Detachment 1, I answered, "Absolutely!" At the same time, I thought, "Why am I doing this?" Everyone knew that Det 1 had the most action by far, was the most remote and was the home of living legends. After proving myself with Det 1, I knew I had found a home. These guys became my family.

Living on a Floating Fortress

Det 1 was based on Sea Float, a group of pontoon barges lashed together and anchored in the middle of the river. The float housed American and Vietnamese military personnel: SEALS, Seawolves, and helicopter gunships. It was a God-forsaken place -- we had more rats than people.

Sea Float was a floating fortress made up of pontoon barges

Life was congested, fast paced, and dangerous. The VC wanted to destroy Sea Float. To protect against sappers *(VC commando units)* and floating mines, concussion grenades were dropped over the side 24/7, often 30 seconds apart. Periodically we found the enemy, armed with C-4, who had been blown up and floated to the top. Despite living conditions, morale was high, leadership was outstanding, and rules and regulations were minimal. That was to my liking.

Life on Det 1 brought us face to face with the toxic defoliant, Agent Orange. From the air, the jungles looked like tiger stripes: strips of triple canopy jungle, next to strips of complete destruction and defoliation. These stripes made it difficult for the VC to get where they wanted to go while under cover. Agent Orange was sprayed along the edges of the river, reducing the enemy's protective cover; consequently, the river was full of the poison.

On Sept 1, 1970 we moved from Sea Float to solid anchor. We enjoyed a shower in the back of our hooch until one day when we were told, "Never use that shower again." We connected the dots – Agent Orange. We've all lived with the implications ever since.

David Smale in a Huey demonstrating the door gunner shooting position.

Scramble the Seawolves

Seawolves excelled at *scrambling*, quickly mobilizing our helicopters. We could go from sleeping to in-the-air in fewer than two minutes and be on station within ten, which made us highly sought after. River patrol boats and SEALS appreciated how quickly we came to their rescue.

I was never wounded, but I was in the helicopter when everyone else was hit. My buddies would say, "Fly with Smale, he's lucky." Others would say, "No, don't fly with Smale. He won't get hit, but you will!"

We would do some pretty crazy stuff. We had a Navy captain with us on a mission when we decided to jump out of the helicopter to chase down a VC and capture him. It was not uncommon, but it was absolutely not allowed. But we did things we weren't allowed to do quite commonly. We finally stopped pursuing him, fearful of booby traps, and had to shoot him. The Navy captain was going crazy and saying he was going to put us in for bravery and the pilot said to him, "Sir, you might want to take a step back." The captain inquired why, and the pilot said, "We didn't do this, sir!"

Worst Day in Vietnam: VC Lake Incident

On September 15, 1970, we were caught in a helicopter trap by the NVA (North Vietnamese Army) 95th regiment. In a helicopter trap, the North Vietnamese Army would surround our forces, leaving an opening to lure in dust-off or gunships. On this occasion, Dust-Off 86, commanded by Lt. Ken Ledford, called for support during an extraction. The Army said no, so Ledford called us.

Our Det 1 gunship scrambled with a Det 6 bird as our fire team sister. Det 6 was shot down immediately. I watched it plummet to the ground and smash into a dike, turning over. I thought, "I can't believe anybody survived that crash."

Then we were shot down. Our pilot, Ltjg Lambert had the presence of mind to steer us into the middle of VC Lake, a decidedly safer place than on the banks with an NVA regiment.

We were under such heavy fire from the shore that the dust-off which we were trying to protect was now attempting to pick *us* up. It took them three passes, braving massive green tracers and a hailstorm of bullets.

Ledford's bird now carried nine of us. I was thinking "My God, we're actually going to live," when the lieutenant said, "We're going down to get your buddies." Under intense fire, he descended as close as he could and his crew chief and one of our pilots jumped out. I also ran to our downed bird where there were two men dead and two who were very badly injured. We got the injured men back to the helicopter. One of them, a good friend, lost his leg.

Now Ledford's bird was carrying eleven guys. Nobody thought we'd make the tree line, but he pulled off a miracle. We were scraping tree limbs on the skids of the helicopter, but we got out. Because of this terrifying incident, my fellow door gunner quit flying immediately. I was back in the air in two days. I knew if I didn't get back quickly, I would never return.

That was one of the worst days of my life; ironically, on the same day several years later, my daughter was born -- one of the best days.

Lt. Ledford was the only Army soldier in the Vietnam War to be awarded a Navy Cross. I received a bronze star with a V for Valor. I extended again and shortly thereafter received a promotion to Second Class Petty Officer.

Smale received a Bronze Star with a V for Valor for his actions on September 15, 1970.

Good and Bad Days of a Seawolf

My friend Mike and I had the day off when we received a call from a Vietnamese Army unit that was being overrun. Det 1 birds were on a mission, so we joined a pilot who had landed in our detachment on a mail run. Under heavy fire, we made ten extractions. Two Det 6 guys were wounded, a pilot was shot in the leg, and a friend had the closest call I'd ever heard of when a round passed between his helmet and his head, exiting out the back of his helmet and creasing his scalp. Still, this was a good day. Several months before I was to go home, my commander asked me to return to HQ to train new people. I thought, "I've been here almost two years, my nerves are shot, and my luck is running out. Maybe that's a good idea."

Impact of Vietnam

My physical arrival in the states occurred at the end of July 1971; mentally coming home took a lot longer. People were not kind and I knew from friends just how much people were against the war. I was in dichotomy because I wasn't in favor of the war either, but I was in favor of being good to my buddies. I enrolled at Michigan State where I met my future wife and we've been together 46 years. I had the good sense to seek counseling. I had my own set of demons. Certain things I'd see and feel over and over. My counselor was remarkable in helping me get back into society. That allowed me to move on with my life.

I think of Vietnam as a chapter in my life, but I have never let it consume me. There's no question that it created enduring friendships and special bonds. I didn't want to go to Vietnam, but I'm a better man and a better leader for it. But these things came at a significant price.

Avid hiders David and Debra Smale, 2018

Peter T. Lillard

New Concept in Amphibious Warfare

Ltjg Peter T. Lillard

The Vietnam War was in full force the winter of 1964, when New Jersey natives Peter T. "Pete" Lillard and his best friend, seniors at Wake Forest University, enlisted in the Navy. "We were getting our degrees in May and we didn't want to be drafted. My friend was hesitant, but later he thanked me profusely, saying that I probably saved his life."

The friends attended OCS (Officer Candidate School) in Newport, RI, and were commissioned as ensigns in November 1965. After two months in Communications School, Lillard was assigned to the USS *Okinawa*, the second *Iwo Jima*-class amphibious assault ship of the United States Navy, home ported in Norfolk, VA. In December 1966, the *Okinawa* was transferred to duty with the Amphibious Force in the Pacific Fleet. On January 24, 1967, Lillard began the long journey to the South China Sea in Vietnam.

The USS Okinawa and Vertical Assault

Lillard's cruise book, "*Okinawa, LPH-3, West 67*, describes the development of the concept of vertical assault:

"With the advent of nuclear weapons, military thinking of the past decades became obsolete. A powerful and highly mobile amphibious force was needed to operate under the threat of nuclear war. Thus, the concept of 'vertical assault' came into being. By this method, most of the assault troops would be taken from an Amphibious Assault Aircraft Carrier, by helicopter, to strategic positions behind enemy lines."

USS Okinawa

The new LPH (Landing Platform Helicopters) provided the command facilities, helicopter operating spaces, and helicopter control and maintenance facilities for assigned forces. Assuming her place in the Pacific Fleet in 1967, the following months were to see *Okinawa* bringing her forces to bear against the enemy in Vietnam. Whenever the Marines landed, *Okinawa* stood in support of her troops ashore.

RPS Custodian and Signals Officer

The USS *Okinawa* carried a Navy crew of 500, fifty officers, and approximately 3,500 Marines, as well as twenty-f single-blade H-34 helicopters, each of which could carry eight fully loaded troops. The ship performed an extremely important support function similar to that of an aircraft carrier for its jet fighters. The helicopters, carried and maintained on the ship, lifted Marines and dropped them in strategic locations, sometimes behind enemy lines, in a relatively safe manner.

Lillard performed three important functions aboard the *Okinawa*, assisting in her mission: as RPS (Registered Publications System) Custodian, Signals Officer, and OOD (officer of the deck). As RPS Custodian, he carried out special functions in connection with communication security and communication and electronic intelligence. "I had a big safe, the size of a small office. lined with key-lists and crypto gear and an Adonis coding machine."

Key lists enabled the decoding of messages and were changed daily. Lillard helicoptered to Da Nang every four to six weeks, where he signed for new key lists and other classified documents, carrying them back to the *Okinawa* in a locked briefcase. Each transmission of code and documents was carefully logged so that Lillard always knew the disposition of the materials.

Lillard (right) in Da Nang on his way to the Communications Center.

The keypads (a pad of key lists) and other classified materials were kept in the safe. Every day Lillard removed the old key list from the teletype machine and inserted a new one. A *burn bag* contained outdated information. "I went down to the furnace in the bowels of the ship, always accompanied by another officer. We both signed a document describing what I threw into the furnace to make sure everything was accounted for."

In his role as Signals Officer, Lillard oversaw communication with other ships using visual methods such as flag hoists (where various combinations of brightly colored flags and pennants are hoisted to send messages), signal lights, and flag waving.

Officer of the Deck

The OOD is the direct representative of the captain during a specific watch, responsible for the ship during that period. At sea, the OOD is stationed on the bridge and oversees navigation and the safety of the ship, unless relieved by the captain or a senior qualified line officer. "The captain tells you where he wants to go and the OOD looks at the chart compass and gives the helmsman the directions – right full rudder, steady to course 009, and so forth. When you get there, the OOD maneuvers the ship so it stays where it's supposed to be. We typically increased speed and made an oval course, maintaining it until all the helicopters had returned. This was necessary to put enough wind over the deck, so they could land more easily than if the ship were still.

Lillard (standing, far left) and the Signals Crew aboard the USS Okinawa

"While on the bridge during transporting the Marines ashore, I would listen to the chatter of the helicopter pilots. They'd announce, 'we're getting incoming fire, we're going up or right or left, we have to get out of here,' etc. It was both fascinating and horrific. One time a helicopter got hit badly with machine gun fire. The pilot made it back, but several rounds had gone into the cockpit. They started bouncing around, off the glass which didn't break. One hit him on the helmet right at his temple, piercing his helmet and nicking his skin. A little drop of blood was running down his face when he climbed out of the helicopter. He was ecstatic. He was a pretty lucky guy!

"We picked up a lot of injuries at night. The wardroom showed nightly movies to Marine and Navy officers. Frequently the movie was interrupted with a message coming over the 1MC, *'medevac, medevac, pilot on duty come to the flight deck right away.'* When that was announced, the three or four Marine officers on duty would jump up and the other Marine officers would jokingly ask them, 'If you don't come back, can I have your radio?'"

When the ship was steaming out in the ocean, the OOD watches were typically four hours each day. "That stopped when we were in a landing operation. During those periods, when more activity was occurring on the bridge, we stood two watches a day, for example noon to 4 p.m. and midnight to 4 a.m." During Lillard's tour in Vietnam, the *Okinawa* participated in eight landings off the South China Sea. These landing operations dropped Marines in locations from the DMZ to an area south of Da Nang.

The Navy crew performed indispensable support for the Marines who carried out the landings. Several of the *Okinawa's* landings included Bear Bite, a search-and-destroy mission near Hue (*pronounced 'way'*), an infiltration route used by North Vietnamese troops; Beaver Cage, a 15-day search-and-destroy operation which disrupted enemy claims to territory 25 miles south of Danang; and, Beacon Gate, *Okinawa's* 6th amphibious assault through an area known to be a Viet Cong stronghold. The fact that the *Okinawa* was available as a floating base made these operations possible.

Underway Replenishment

Having to remain on station for long periods of time depleted the *Okinawa's* fuel supply and required that they receive underway replenishment of oil, water and supplies, rendezvousing with a tanker at sea. Lillard was one of four officers who stood OOD during these refueling operations. Underway replenishment is risky since the two ships must hold to precisely the same course and speed for a long period of time. A slight steering error on the part of one of the ships could cause a collision or separate the transfer lines and fuel hoses. Thus, the refueling team was a highly specialized detail. Experienced and qualified crew were required during this process, paying constant attention to the ship's course and speed.

The ship's captain usually took the con (assumed the responsibility of steering the ship) during refueling operations, often on the wing of the bridge in order to get a better view of the gap between the two ships. He shouted instructions to Lillard who would relay them to the helmsman on the bridge.

Lillard recalled one particularly tense refueling. The *Okinawa*, as the guide ship, was supposed to maintain course and speed while the tanker adjusted its course and speed to sustain the proper tension in the connecting oil hose. "For some reason, the tanker was having difficulty staying abreast of us. He would get back three or four yards, causing more tension, or he'd move forward a few yards. The result could have been either separating the hose or collision."

In this instance, the captain was so far on the right wing of the bridge that he was looking at the compass at an angle that indicated compass degrees off by several degrees. The result was that the ships were moving closer together. Lillard recognized what was happening and walked over to the captain, quietly explaining that he was reading the compass incorrectly because of the angle. The captain moved back to where he could observe the compass directly and the replenishment was completed successfully.

Back in the USA

Lillard's reception in San Diego was not as confrontational as those received by his Army and Marine comrades. However, "you didn't want to talk about your military experience with strangers. Someone always took umbrage with what was going on in Vietnam. I grew my hair back as quickly as possible."

Recovery of Apollo Six

The USS *Okinawa* was the prime recovery ship for the Apollo 6 unmanned space mission. On April 4, 1968, Lillard watched as the spacecraft command module was hoisted aboard, 375 nautical miles north of Honolulu, Hawaii. "The module landed fairly close to the ship – helicopters got to it within minutes. It was fascinating to be on the bridge and listen to NASA bigwigs talking to the captain about the mission, and their concerns and plans for future manned flights."

Lillard left the Navy the winter of 1968 and remembers being glued to the television as the country witnessed the violence and protests against the Vietnam War which occurred during the Democratic National Convention in Chicago.

Minesweepers off the Coast of New Jersey

Recovering Apollo Six space capsule aboard the USS Okinawa, April 4, 1968.

Several years later, the ocean again called to Lillard. After some research, he learned that the United States Naval Reserve operated two minesweepers out of Perth Amboy, just an hour's drive from his New Jersey home. For the next five years, he joined local reserve crews one weekend a month and two weeks in the summer, conducting periodic exercises up and down the east coast, from Rhode Island to South Carolina. Lillard was promoted to Lieutenant Commander by the time he left the service, including reserve time.

After the Navy, Lillard enjoyed a financial career in trust administration, where he met his wife, Marjorie, who was the daughter of one of his clients. Today they enjoy the activities of their five children and 11 grandchildren. Peter loves the game of golf, although he admits he's playing less these days. His hobby is building and shooting the flintlock musket, the most important weapon of the Revolutionary War.

Lessons of Vietnam

"I think everyone should serve in the military for at least six months. You learn accountability and time management. You also learn to lead by example. If you do the right thing, people under you tend to do the right thing. When I was in Vietnam, and when I first got home, I thought it was good to be there. As I get older, I'm not as sure. We lost more than 58,000 American lives."

Peter and his granddaughter Eleanor, 2018

Earl Flynn Trimnal

War in the Underground Battlefields of Vietnam

Pvt. First Class Earl Flynn Trimnal
Boot Camp, 1967

Building tunnels and forts with his friends in the swamps near Georgetown, S.C. offered young Earl "Flynn" Trimnal excellent conditioning for one of the jobs he would someday assume in Vietnam – that of a *tunnel rat*.

"From the time I was about six years old, I wanted to join the Marine Corps. My dad was in the Navy at Utah Beach in Normandy and I grew up wanting to serve my country. For three years, beginning in 9th grade, I worked after school, earning money to pay for summer school classes so I could graduate early. I wanted to get to Vietnam to help my country. I went to live with my grandparents when I was about twelve. My grandma was very strict. For example, she had a switch at the dinner table, and she'd whack us if we put our elbows on the table. Because of this discipline, I excelled in boot camp and was one of three in my platoon of 85 to make Private First Class."

The 17-year-old high school graduate entered the Marine Corps in October 1967. His training took him from boot camp at Parris Island to Camp Lejeune and then Camp Geiger for advanced training in the 106 recoilless rifle, flame throwers, and demolition. In Okinawa, Trimnal continued his training. The day he turned 18, he was on a plane to Vietnam.

Congratulations, You're a Tunnel Rat!

Trimnal was assigned to the 3rd Reconnaissance Battalion, 26th Marines. "When I got off the chopper, this big old gunnery sergeant kept looking at me and scratching his head. I said, 'PFC Trimnal reporting as ordered sir,' and he said, 'Congratulations, Private Trimnal! You're our new tunnel rat.'"

Tunnel Rats: American, Australian and New Zealand military soldiers entering Viet Cong (VC) tunnels. Photo credit: Black Ink Clothing.

During the Vietnam War, Viet Cong Communist guerrilla troops dug tens of thousands of tunnels, using them for intelligence work and as hiding places after ambushes. U.S. tunnel rats were combat engineers on underground search and destroy missions: small, thin and skilled in hand-to-hand combat, armed only with flashlights, knives and pistols.

In the tunnels Trimnal found booby traps such as grenades, mines and punji sticks, venomous snakes, rats, huge spiders and scorpions. Sometimes poisonous gases were used. "I lived in constant fear of what I would encounter or who I would meet with each foot that I crawled, knowing I could set off a booby-trap at any moment.

"When they found a tunnel, they called me in. Before I went into the tunnels I thought, 'It's just you and me, Lord. Let's go.' Usually they tied a rope to my foot, so they could pull me out if I got shot. Several times I had to throw a grenade because there were people back there. The life expectancy for a tunnel rat is about seven seconds, but I was never injured while in the tunnel.

"A young Vietnamese boy showed me a lifesaving technique. He gave me a small glass mirror on a telescope, which could be angled in different directions. The Viet Cong put curves in the tunnels for ambushes, or they dug deep holes and filled them with water, in order to hear us coming. I'd get to a turn and put the angled mirror down to see around the corner. Then lob a grenade in there. I still have that mirror. It saved my life many times."

Transfer to Reconnaissance

Flynn Trimnal excelled at tunnel work and eventually was transferred to Force Recon (Force Reconnaissance.) Force Recon operated behind enemy lines, surveilling the enemy and providing military intelligence to Marine command. Remaining undetected was crucial.

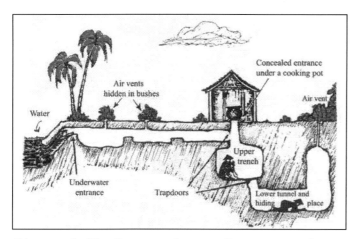

Diagram of a Viet Cong tunnel system. Every curve and turn was a potential death trap for a tunnel rat.

Trimnal and his radioman, Calvin, scouted ahead of the battalion, providing information about enemy activities while avoiding direct combat and detection. The two men worked together as a team, one tall, dark and lanky, the other short, pale and compact. "They put us out in the jungle many miles ahead, and while we were returning, we were very cautious, always watching. If we saw movement, we avoided contact and called in artillery. Calvin and I went on many recon missions and we were very successful.

"One day the VC spotted us. I told Calvin, 'let's go,' and we started running. They were lobbing mortars in on us. I was shorter than he was, and I could get down lower. A mortar landed near us and messed him up pretty bad. Rather than leave him there, I grabbed him by the collar and dragged him up behind some rocks. The radio was still on his back, so I called it in. I kept talking and firing my rifle and suddenly, I heard a tank. I knew it was ours and it was a good sound. But Calvin didn't make it. He died. He was from Wilmington, but I didn't even know his last name.

"After Calvin died, I went crazy. I felt that he was my responsibility. He had done his job and I should have done mine better. *Crazy* became my nickname. Everyone wanted to be with me because they knew I was there for business. I just didn't care."

Recon team and friends, radioman Calvin and Flynn Trimnal

Promotion to Squad Leader

After Calvin died, Trimnal was promoted to Sergeant and made a squad leader. "One time at 1:30 a.m. we were about 15 miles from our compound when they called us on our radio. They estimated 150 North Vietnamese regulars in our area. We were instructed to avoid contact if possible. I pulled my men into a small thicket. I could see an enemy soldier's feet and if he'd taken one more step, he would have stepped on my rifle. He stayed there for what seemed like five hours but was probably about two minutes, and then he walked on. They never saw us. We waited until they got away, and then we called in artillery. The next morning there were at least 75 enemy dead.

"Our job was always to know where the enemy was, and to call it in. Sometimes with a squad, we would engage if we had to. But after Calvin, I felt my first job was to take care of my men."

Above: Trimal launching a mortar.
Top right: Home Sweet Home: Trimnal's hooch.
Bottom right: Trimnal and a South Vietnamese civilian driver

Three Times Wounded in Action

Trimnal was wounded twice and sent back into action. "The third time I was injured, my buddies and I were ambushed near an Esso plant. We pushed them back and then pulled a sweep to pick up bodies. I came across a VC in a bomb crater, but I'd run out of rounds in my magazine. I jumped in there and we did a bayonet shuffle. A log had flopped down, and he was against the tree. I bayonetted him, and it went right through to that tree. Another VC came at me and bayoneted me in the side. I reached in for my ka-bar (knife) and got him in the throat. I don't even remember that. When I woke up, I was on the USS *New Orleans* and I thought, 'I'm still alive.' My two friends came up to me and said, 'Hey you'd do anything to get out of the bush.'"

No Easy Transition Home

Trimnal recovered on the USS *New Orleans* during the two weeks it took to get back to San Diego where he spent a month rehabilitating and two months of light duty. "When it was time to go home, I went to the airport, proud of my sergeant stripes and my medals. I was in my uniform with my sea bag. A woman came out of nowhere, wearing something that looked like a flour sack, and spit on me and called me a baby killer. I didn't want to resort to violence, so I went into the bathroom and changed into civilian clothes. I bought a first-class ticket home. After that, I never wore my uniform off base."

Trimnal left the service in 1972. In 1967, near the end of his stint in boot camp, the Secret Service had interviewed Trimnal for a position in the Presidential Helicopter Squadron. He told them that he wanted to be a Marine to help the South Vietnamese people. The service suggested that if he survived Vietnam, he should pursue the position again. "At that time, I had really wanted to be in the Marine Corps; but after Vietnam, I realized the government didn't take care of us, which threw that dream out the window. We did all that fighting and dying. We fought our hearts out and the government just handed it all away – just picked up and left. I'd had enough."

Like many other returning Vietnam veterans, Trimnal received no debriefing, no counseling, and no preparation for his return home. He found the transition back to "normal" life almost impossible; in fact, he camped in the forest for 30 days, eating squirrels and fish and trading for supplies. He distrusted the government, which had turned its back on him, and encountered numerous readjustment difficulties. Unable to obtain work in South Carolina ("I was told, 'I aint hiring no crazy Vietnam vet!'") Trimnal moved to Florida and eventually found a job washing dishes.

"I just didn't care about anything. I would ride 150 mph on my motorcycle and not even think about it. Just to feel the breeze over my hair." After a failed marriage, Trimnal's shattered life began a reversal when he met a young woman named Jude and they began a friendship that was based on faith and love that would weather all storms. They have been married for 27 years.

Getting Help for PTSD and Moral Injury

Post-traumatic stress disorder, once referred to by terms such as shell shock and battle fatigue, affected approximately 30% of men and 27% of women at some point following their Vietnam experience. Many veterans, especially those like Trimnal, who experienced high levels of combat exposure, continue to suffer the effects of PTSD. In effect, they are still living the war.

Moral injury, a concept relatively new to psychology, can be defined as a profound change in or betrayal of one's sense of right or wrong…emotions felt by many veterans and active service members in response to the ethical and moral challenges of war. [*GoodTherapy Blog*]

Trimnal's symptoms were severe. "I tried to take AutoCAD in college in Charleston. It was near an Air Force Base and when those planes and jets would fly over, I'd flash back. The instructor's mouth would be moving but I'd be hearing bombs and explosions and mortars going off and I could see the flashes. I had to drop the course."

"I didn't want to admit there was anything wrong with me. I was a highly trained Marine. I felt ashamed that I'd been wounded – that I wasn't a good Marine. It wasn't until 1995 that I finally went to the VA hospital in Asheville. Every time someone came into the room, or dropped something, or a phone rang, I jumped. A psychologist asked me why I wore camouflage. I said, 'I feel ready, alert.' They took me to a room with a big round table with eight people sitting around it. There was one vacant chair near the door. I picked up that chair and took it all the way around to the other side of the table and said, 'What do you want to know?' After a brief conversation, I was told I had PTSD. I asked, 'What's that?'"

Trimnal and his doctors eventually found the appropriate medication which prevents agitation and takes the edge off for him, which has enabled him to quit smoking and drinking. Most importantly, he joined a PTSD class. Relief came at last when he joined a *Moral Injury Group* which helps veterans who live with guilt and emotional trauma.

"Two other guys and I went through it all together. We were supposed to dissolve after the class, but it helped us so much that we continued." The Moral Injury Group meets every Monday at the VA. "I love them, they're my brothers."

Advice for PTSD Sufferers

When asked what advice he would offer veterans suffering from PTSD, Trimnal replied promptly, "Admit you have a problem. Then find help. If you're experiencing thoughts of killing people, of cutting their heads off and putting them on a stick in front of your house, you need to go to the VA." Old feelings still crop up, but Trimnal has his friends, his wife and his counselor. And his faith. "I carried that grudge for so many years. Jude and I listen to Charles Stanley in the morning. One day he said, 'For God to forgive you, you've got to forgive others.' And I thought, 'Oh my God.' And the anger and hate left me, just like that."

Flynn's wife, Jude Trimnal, offered words of encouragement from a veteran's wife's perspective. "Being married to someone with PTSD is still difficult at times. It's impossible to understand all that Flynn went through. In the beginning I didn't handle it very well. It was like living with two different people. I still try to be with him a lot. I never know when a flashback will occur. These guys were trained to become the way they needed to be for warfare. Flynn was wounded three times. And when he came back to California on the ship's hospital after being bayonetted, they basically just threw him out on the street and said 'Go home. Go get a library card. Get back to your life.'

"But the VA hospital is finally working to help veterans and their families. They have a class for women living with vets with PTSD which I attended for three weeks. Just like Flynn in his class, I realized I wasn't alone. It's important for us to realize that they're not like this on purpose. PTSD is a condition they have. We must deal with it and hopefully make it better. How we handle it is important. We must fight PTSD together."

Coming Full Circle

Flynn Trimnal's story has several happy endings. His wife, Jude, is his best friend and advocate. "Sometimes it's still hard," she admits. "But he's a good man. When he has setbacks, he keeps trying and doesn't give up." Trimnal's constant companion, an eleven-year-old terrier mix named Penny, offers comfort and a calming effect when Trimnal feels anxious. And life is never boring, always fun when grandsons Parker and Harrison visit.

And there is another Calvin in Trimnal's life.

In October, Trimnal and 80 other Vietnam veterans took the Blue Ridge Honor Flight to Washington, DC, where they enjoyed a day of sightseeing and a hero's welcome when they returned home. On the return flight to Asheville, veterans received letters written by local school children, thanking them for their service. One of Trimnal's letters was from an 8th grade boy named Calvin. Trimnal couldn't believe his eyes. He responded to the young man and Calvin sent several meaningful letters. "I feel as if everything has come full circle."

Flynn takes great joy in visits from his grandsons Harrison (left) and Parker.

Jude and Flynn Trimnal at a dress-up Beatles music concert, 2018

> To learn more about PTSD and moral injury treatment options, self-help tools, and resources, call 800-273-TALK (8255) and press #1 to speak to someone who will direct callers to the assistance requested.

Welcome Home, Brother

Lt. Col. David B. Grant, USAF (Ret.)
Phantom Pilot and Prisoner of War

Captain David Grant in an F-4 Phantom at MacDill AFB, Tampa, 1970

On June 24, 1972, U.S. Air Force Captain David B. Grant was flying a mission from Thailand into conflict-ridden North Vietnam when his F-4 Phantom took a direct hit and exploded. The fuselage separated as both Grant and his back-seater, Bill, ejected through the fireball. They landed without injury, about two miles apart. They did not see each other again until days later when they were cellmates in the infamous North Vietnamese prison known to American POWs as the Hanoi Hilton.

Grant and his father, Colonel A.G. Grant, share a dubious distinction. As a young lieutenant flying B-17's during WWII, A.G. was shot down over Belgium and spent a year and a half as a prisoner of war in Stalag Luft I. A.G. and David are the only father (WWII) and son (Vietnam War) to have been POWs from those conflicts.

Grant had not intended to follow so closely in his father's footsteps; in fact, it was his father who advised him against becoming a pilot. Grant had graduated from the University of Chattanooga in 1965 when he learned he'd received his draft notice and immediately enlisted in the Air Force. "I wanted to be a hospital administrator, but because of a pilot shortage, they made me a pilot."

After attending Officer Training School in San Antonio, Grant and his new bride, Betsy, moved to Laredo Texas for flight training. Upon graduation, his group had orders for Vietnam. But in January 1968, the USS *Pueblo* was attacked and captured by North Korea. Vietnam orders were cancelled, and they went to Japan.

There Grant met Lt. John Barker *[page 73]* and was assigned as his GIB (guy-in-back), flying F-4 Phantoms. "John had a huge influence on my flying career. We spent about 70% of our time in South Korea." From Japan, Grant returned to MacDill Air Force Base in Tampa where he upgraded to Aircraft Commander (guy-in-front). Once again, he received orders to Da Nang which were changed, and the Grants went to the Philippines.

Flying Low from Da Nang

In 1972, President Nixon authorized increased air strikes on North Vietnam targets. "Our assignment in the Philippines was curtailed and I again had orders for Da Nang. I had seven days' notice to get Betsy and the boys back to the states and depart. I arrived in Da Nang on April 1, 1972.

"When I got to Da Nang, I knew I was in a war. My first night, I heard a siren. I went out onto the metal stairs in the back of our quarters, standing out there with a drink in my hand, when a fuel truck took a rocket. It just went "boom" right in front of me. And I thought, 'My God, this is really war.' We experienced rocket attacks almost every night in Da Nang. There was a guy who sat on the side of a mountain and shot at us as we came in to land. We knew we were in a combat zone at Da Nang.

"Flying from Da Nang was rewarding from a pilot's point of view. We flew a lot of close air support for our guys using ordnance that required low-level delivery for accuracy. Flying at 1,000 to 2,000 feet, we often smelled the gun smoke and watched the enemy scattering or even shooting at us, even though we were going 450 knots. When successful, we received some rewarding calls relayed back through the forward air controller that said 'Thank you! You saved our butts.'

Da Nang Air Base. *"We experienced rocket attacks almost every night in Da Nang."*

"I had one mission where the North Vietnamese Army were positioned on the 2nd floor of a plantation house. They had our guys pinned down in the front yard behind a stone wall. From my plane, which was level with the 2nd floor window, I was able to strafe and clear the enemy from the building. I was so low that my jet's exhaust dusted our guys."

Captured and a Painful Journey

In June, Grant's wing moved from Da Nang to Takhli, Thailand. He and Bill, his GIB, were shot down at 4 p.m. on June 24, 1972 on their first mission out of Takhli, about forty miles from Hanoi. "They tried to shoot me as I parachuted down and were fairly close when I landed, so I hid under a very dense bush on a steep incline. I dug in a little so I wouldn't slide down. I spent the night that way, with creatures crawling all over me. The North Vietnamese were less than 50 yards away."

In the morning, the enemy began their search and found Grant's hiding place. "They did a 'ready, aim, fire' and several of them shot into the bush. Then they waited. Then another 'ready, aim, fire.' One shot hit me in the foot. They came into the brush and were shocked that I was alive when I rolled my head around and looked up at them.

"They tied my arms in back around a bamboo pole. I had a hole in my foot and hadn't had any water. Then we started a hike. This was June in the jungle, and it took about four-and-a-half hours to get down the mountain. In the villages, they stirred up the crowd and the villagers struck me with sticks and rocks. Eventually a militia guy took over and beat me up. He stuck his automatic between my eyes and pulled the trigger. It clicked. Then they put me in an open field, all tied up, formed a line and did the *ready, aim, fire* thing again, for another mock execution.

"We continued through villages. In each one I was beaten. Finally, we arrived at a larger village where they held a night-time kangaroo-court trial. I was on my knees with a bayonet on either side of my head and I made the mistake of smiling at the woman who held one of the bayonets. She made sure the blood kept seeping from my temple. I was convicted as a war criminal and thrown into a little hut. They gave me some slush with rice and fish that was hard to keep down."

The next morning, they released Grant to the regulars who put a bag over his head and tossed him onto the back of a truck for the journey to Hanoi. The road was in terrible condition and each bump and jostle brought agonizing pain to his injured foot.

Heartbreak Hotel

In Hanoi, prison guards freed Grant's arms and threw him into a small room. "I stayed on the floor. After four days of interrogation and beatings, they put me in a small cell in the section of the prison called *Heartbreak Hotel*. The dingy 5'x 7' cells held two concrete slabs with shackles on the end. I lay there with no idea where I was, but it must have been Sunday because I heard some Americans singing.

"I hopped or crawled wherever I went, and the guard, unsympathetic because it slowed him down, *encouraged* me with his rifle butt or his foot. The entire time I was there, nobody ever addressed my foot. I received zero medical help.

"Because I couldn't walk, they put Bill in with me. We were together the rest of the time. After five days (which seemed like two years), the guards told us to put on our long pajamas. They tied us up, put bags over our heads, and took six of us to a news conference. At that point, Betsy learned from the foreign press that I was alive."

At the news conference, Grant received a small towel to wrap around the filthy rag on his foot and a crutch which proved useful in more ways than one. "Eventually I was able to walk on my heel, but I faked that I couldn't walk. I got fast on the crutch. I put it against the wall and climbed on it to reach the bars where I used hand signals to communicate with guys across the way. Bill watched the door. When he spotted a guard, he got in his area quickly and I jumped down, grabbed the crutch, and did the same.

"By the end of July my leg was discolored up to just below the knee, with long grey/green streaks. My foot was huge and a strange color. I think the interrogations may have helped, because the enemy started each interrogation by stomping or jamming anything that was injured. That kept my foot bleeding and may have helped clean the wound, because the water was filthy. Finally, a guard gave me two small white tablets and eventually the infection subsided."

Eating and Staying Sane

Eventually Grant and Bill moved to a larger room with other POWs. They received two small meals a day. Breakfast was tea and a half loaf of bread. "The bread had things in it, like bug parts and rat poop. We ate everything because it was probably the only protein we got. The tea was a little bit of dirty water and maybe a tea leaf. In the afternoon we received tea, another piece of bread and a bowl of soup. The summer fare was pumpkin soup. I knew it was pumpkin because they were stored on the floor in our room. Huge rats gnawed at them and they were moldy. The broth was orangish water. A shred of pumpkin in your soup was a treasure. You'd look at it and say, *filet mignon*!

"Most days included five-to-ten minutes outside where we scooped the mosquito larva off the top of a horse trough and poured cold water, no soap, on ourselves with a bucket. We washed our shorts and put them back on again wet.

"For entertainment, we recounted our histories. As we accumulated more people, we held classes and played games such as Jeopardy. We kept score using pieces of straw, or in our heads. We took turns telling stories, which was my favorite activity. Generally, it turned out to be about a date we'd had in our hometown: how we picked her up, where we went to dinner, what we'd had to eat. Eventually, the guard ordered us to go to bed, but the light always stayed on. To this day, I can't sleep with the light on.

"The prison was hot in the summer; we were always sweating. And there was very little water. The winter was miserable. We didn't need our mosquito nets when it got cold, so we used them as a cover. We were all freezing and shivering, and when we shivered, the bed boards rattled. It was a symphony of teeth chattering and bed boards rattling.

"In the big room we had a 50-gallon drum that had two heavy wires across it which came down to be the handle. There was a 'throne' up there. We walked up eight steps to a concrete platform with a hole in the middle. That was our out-house.

"The fun part was moving the drum to empty it. We eased it out and tried to keep it from splashing. Two guys of even height -- a Navy guy and I -- carried the drum on a bamboo pole that hung between us, walking in unison to assure that it didn't slosh too much. We carried it into the courtyard, pulled up the grate, and dumped it. And we always tried to get a little on the guard. I can't believe we did that. We washed up afterwards, but once again, no soap."

Keeping the Home Fires Burning

During Grant's imprisonment, Betsy coped at home. Grant believes he had the easy job. "All I had to do was stay alive. Betsy had the hard job of caring for our two small sons, David and Stephen, tending the home alone, and worrying about me." Betsy responded, "We were blessed to know within five days that he was alive. I was fortunate at home in Chattanooga, lovingly supported by family, friends and church. And, as his grandmother said, we waited with bated breath."

Left: Betsy preparing a CARE package for her husband, with sons David and Stephen.

Release and Homecoming

In mid-December 1972, with the failure of peace talks, President Nixon announced the beginning of a massive bombing campaign. The first mission was December 18, 1972. "We called them the *Christmas bombings* and we finally knew that there was hope." The bombings continued until the North Vietnamese agreed to resume peace talks. The Paris Peace Accords were signed in January 1973. From February to April, missions departed Hanoi, bringing the POWs out. Groups of prisoners were released based on length of time in prison and medical condition. The North Vietnamese moved the more recent POWs from the Hanoi Hilton to a place called The Zoo, a prison on the other side of Hanoi which had been an old French cinema. POWs from the Chinese border, such as Ray Alcorn *[page 39]*, returned to the Hanoi Hilton and were released first. Grant's flight home was second to last, departing Hanoi on March 28, 1973.

Captain David Grant arriving in Chattanooga for the city's Welcome Home ceremony.

"They put us on a bus and took us out to a C-141. We were all very antsy, knowing that they could stop the release or even shoot us down. Nobody was comfortable until we were over the water. Then it was great."

On Grant's previous trips home, he'd encountered strong antiwar sentiment as he flew into San Francisco. "I was on flights with guys that had been jerked out of combat, still in their combat fatigues. They were stinking and dirty and had just been out shooting people, and suddenly they're in an airplane coming home. The guys were still in combat mode which is when your senses are up and you're ready to pounce. And suddenly, they're being verbally and sometimes physically abused by their countrymen."

Grant's last trip home was different. The POWs were flown to the Philippines for medical treatment and debriefing. Grant was greeted at Clark AFB by former squadron members, including his cousin Rhae Mozley and her husband Don. "The guys all wanted steaks and a dozen eggs. My friends came up to visit me and they'd shake my hand and press a little bottle of Old Grandad into it." After several days of rest, the former POWs returned to the U.S. in new uniforms to a heroes' welcome, including hundreds of yellow ribbons.

Betsy and Dave Grant at a press conference in Chattanooga, Tennessee in April 1973. POWs, unlike other returning Vietnam warriors, received heroes' welcomes.

Aftermath

Grant remained in the Air Force after the war, retiring as Lt. Col. in 1994. He and Betsy have three sons, David, Stephen, and Robert, and nine grandchildren. Their favorite activities are family-focused, including Cousin Camp when all the grandchildren come for a visit.

When asked about PTSD, Grant replied, "We didn't admit to it, because if we did we'd lose our flight pay. They'd ground us because they'd think we weren't stable. I suppressed it. If I got into pressure in my job, I'd go out into the garage and lie on the concrete floor and think 'things aren't so bad.'"

Dave and Betsy at the "Return to Freedom" 45th reunion, 2018

In August 2018, Dave and more than 120 Vietnam War POWs and their families gathered in Frisco, Texas for a *Return to Freedom* 45th reunion. The reunion was hosted by developer Ross Perot Jr. and a veterans' organization.

In the Grant home, a brass plaque expresses the sentiments that husband and wife hold dear. It reads:

You have never lived 'til you have almost died. And for those who fight for it, life has a flavor the protected will never know.

Made in the USA
Monee, IL
03 March 2020